Dracula

– Celebrating 100 years –

Edited by:

Leslie Shepard

Albert Power

MENTOR PRESS

First Published in 1997 by

MENTOR Press
43 Furze Road,
Sandyford Industrial Estate,
Dublin 18,
Republic of Ireland.

Tel: (353)-1- 295 2112 / 3   Fax: (353)-1- 295 2114

Edited by: Leslie Shepard
Albert Power

The Publishers wish to thank the following
for permission to reproduce illustrations
Don Conroy
Mary Connolly
Roger Conroy
Claudia Andrei

Cover Illustration by Jonathan Barry
Postage stamps reproduced by kind permission of An Post © 1997

Design and Layout: Tony Hetherington
Kathryn McKinney

Printed by ColourBooks Ltd., Dublin.

ISBN: 0 947548 84 X

1 3 5 7 9 10 8 6 4 2

CONTENTS

ABOUT THE EDITORS

LESLIE SHEPARD

Leslie Shepard is an author, folklorist, former documentary film director. He has published books on Street Literature (the penny balladsheets and chapbooks which were the literature of poor people before cheap printing), and also lectured and written on comparative religion and the occult.

He edited three editions of the massive *Encyclopedia of Occultism and Parapsychology* (3rd ed, 2 vols, Detroit, 1991), a standard reference work in American libraries. His anthology, *The Dracula Book of Great Vampire Stories* (1977), was one of the choices of the Book of the Month Club in the U.S. He also edited *The Dracula Book of Great Horror Stories*.

He has been closely connected with Hindu communities and he spent a year living in the Himalayas, studying yoga, religious philosophy, and Indian music. He has edited English editions of works on Indian religion, and was a script adviser on the dance-drama *Nritya Natika Ramayana* (Indo-British Cultural Exchange, 1981). His long-play record album *The Sounds of Yoga-Vedanta: Documentary of Life in an Indian Ashram* was issued by Folkways Records, New York (since acquired by the Smithsonian Institution).

He has featured on radio and television and lectured at various ecumenical religious conferences. He is Chairman of the Bram Stoker Society, Dublin.

ALBERT POWER

Albert Power is Treasurer and Registrar of the Bram Stoker Society and is also editor of the annual *Bram Stoker Society Journal*. He has contributed regularly to the newsletter and journal of the Bram Stoker Society and has presented a paper each year at the annual Bram Stoker International Summer School in Clontarf, Dublin since its inception in 1991. An early achievement of his was the successful launching of a Gothic stage melodrama written by himself, in Irish, in Carraroe, Co. Galway in June 1976. He has also featured on radio and television in connection with Bram Stoker and the supernatural tradition in literature.

He is a solicitor and currently works as Director of Education with the Law Society of Ireland and as Principal of the Law Society's Law School. He has written for the *Irish Current Law Statutes Annotated*, the *Industrial Relations DataBank* and the *Solicitors' Gazette*.

Bram Stoker
1906

INTRODUCTION

One hundred years ago, an Irish author created a vampire Count who travelled from a ruined Transylvanian castle to Whitby, in England. Since then, Count Dracula has travelled through some forty different countries, his journey chronicled in over twenty different languages.

According to folk superstition, vampires live indefinitely as long as they can feast on the blood of living victims. Although in Stoker's thrilling story Dracula is exterminated, yet he continues to live on all over the world in hundreds of movies, plays, and academic studies. This dread phantom is now as firmly rooted in popular imagination as Frankenstein's monster, or the more benign Sherlock Holmes and other enduring fictional characters.

When the book first appeared in 1897, some people found it too terrifying and perhaps vulgar. The highbrow journal Athenaeum sniffed: "*Dracula* is highly sensational, but is wanting in the constructive art as well as in the highest literary sense. It reads at times like a mere series of grotesquely incredible events . . ." A critic in The Bookman stated grudgingly: "A summary of the work would shock and disgust; but we must own that, though here and there in the course of the tale we hurried over things with repulsion, we read nearly the whole with rapt attention." Other writers were more generous. The Daily Mail compared "This weird, powerful and horrible story" with "such tales as 'The Mysteries of Udolpho', 'Frankenstein', 'Wuthering Heights', 'The Fall of the House of Usher' ", while Arthur Conan Doyle, creator of the equally immortal Sherlock Holmes, wrote: "I think it is the very best story of diablerie which I have read for many years. It is really wonderful how with so much exciting interest over so long a book that there is never an anticlimax."

In Stoker's book, Count Dracula exclaims: "You think to baffle me, you - with your pale faces all in a row . . . You think you have left me without a place to rest; but I have more. My revenge is just begun! I spread it over centuries, and time is on my side!"

One hundred years later, *Dracula* continues to exert a powerful influence in an age which has long outgrown the narrow conventions of Victorian England. The present collection of studies on the book and its author reviews some of the many popular and scholarly aspects of a literary phenomenon.

One good reason for the enduring popularity of Stoker's novel, written in limited spare time in between strenuous labours as Theatre Manager to the great actor, Henry Irving, lies precisely in its appeal on so many different levels. It appeals equally to the ordinary man and woman in the street and to the academic, analysing and discussing structural motifs, psychological implications, and archetypal significance. We have reflected this wide range of interest in the choice of essays by various contributors in the present book. Inevitably there is some occasional repetition or overlap of information, but this must be seen in the context of the viewpoints of individual contributors. These essays discuss the nature of the vampire, superstition and belief in the supernatural, the creation of Stoker's Dracula, and the character and life of Stoker himself, including his important work in the theatre with actor Henry Irving, Stoker's little known talents as a journalist, and the place which his famous novel occupies in the literature of the Gothic Novel and the specifically Irish supernatural tale. Dracula has been widely recognised as one of the most influential novels of the supernatural.

Above all, Stoker revived an ancient mythology of the vampire, an evil creature as greatly feared as the devil in Christian theology. There continues to be much evil in modern life, and a story of the constant struggle to defeat its power is always a valuable allegory.

Dracula was not the first vampire story. Aside from the rather slight *The Vampyre* of John William Polidori in 1819, pride of place goes to the Irish writer Joseph Sheridan Le Fanu, with his story *Carmilla* (1871), which preceded and partly influenced Stoker's story, but *Dracula* is certainly one of the most famous Irish novels of all time.

Surprisingly Ireland has often been slow to recognise its own literary heroes. It took several decades for writers like James Joyce and Samuel Beckett to become ranked as national assets, while in the case of Bram Stoker, the activities of the Bram Stoker Society and the International Bram Stoker Summer School were often reported by Irish journalists in a context of weak jokes of the "Fangs awfully" kind. But there are now signs that Stoker is being treated seriously.

With the present centenary of first publication of *Dracula*, Stoker is being recognised as an important national figure. A new Irish language translation of his book is being issued to celebrate the centenary, while An Post is issuing commemorative postage stamps in conjunction with similar issues in the U.S., Canada and Britain. Film units from the U.S., France, Germany and Japan have been filming television documentaries on the Irish roots of *Dracula*, while the tourist industry, aware of the booming tourist trade in Romania (Transylvania), is recognising that Stoker was a Dublin man.

A century after his influential book, and 150 years after his birth in a Dublin suburb, Stoker is at last coming into his own in Ireland.

Leslie Shepard
Albert Power

1. ARE THERE SUCH THINGS AS VAMPIRES ?

~ Ralph Shirley ~

The following Editorial by the Hon. Ralph Shirley (1865-1946) is from the November 1924 issue of the journal *Occult Review*, which Shirley founded in 1905 and edited for twenty-one years. It was undoubtedly the best occult journal ever published, and included articles from many famous contributors, including Lady Archibald Campbell, A.E. Waite, Hereward Carrington, Oliver Fox, and others. Shirley was the brother of the eleventh Earl Ferrers and a direct descendant of Robert Devereux, Earl of Essex. He was educated at Winchester, and New College, Oxford University. From 1892-1925 he was director of William Rider & Son, the foremost British publishers of literature on occultism, mysticism, New Thought, astrology, and psychical research and was Stoker's main U.K. publisher from 1911 onwards. He was also Vice-President of the International Institute for Psychic Investigation.

In September 1933, the title of the journal was changed briefly to *The London Forum*, but resumed the title *Occult Review* until 1948, when it then became *Rider's Review* before eventually ceasing publication. In addition to his own books on astrology, reincarnation, and the life of Abraham Lincoln, Shirley published many important works by other writers, some of which were reprinted in the 1960s by University Books, Inc., New York, becoming key items in the occult revival. Shirley died December 29, 1946.

Modern scientific discovery on the one hand, and the investigations in connection with psychic phenomena on the other, have rendered credible today many ancient records which were, until recently, dismissed as legendary romance. The point may be raised, in this connection, whether the phenomena observed at materialising séances and in particular the discovery of the peculiar properties of ectoplasm, will not open the door to a reconsideration of the long-rejected belief in vampires. It may, indeed, be argued that we hear nothing of vampires nowadays, and that if there were vampires in the past

we should surely still meet with them, if only rarely and at long intervals. In speaking of vampires, I am not, of course, referring to the generally admitted belief in the power of one person to vampirize another by draining his or her vitality in normal conditions of association either through frequent social intercourse, or more effectually through two people sleeping in the same bed, one of whom is lacking in the vitality of which the other possesses an abundance. This belief would be admitted, it may be presumed, by most medical men at the present day. What I allude to is the supposed existence of the living-dead in the tomb, the vampire, that is, as it is defined in *Webster's Dictionary*, as "a blood-sucking ghost or reanimated body of a dead person; a soul or reanimated body of a dead person believed to come from the grave and wander about by night sucking the blood of persons asleep, thereby causing their death." [1]

Bram Stoker's novel, *Dracula*, has popularised this superstition, if indeed it is merely superstition, and it must be at once admitted that a vampire exercising the activities ascribed by the novelist to Dracula has no parallel even in the weirdest legends of the Slavonic races. We are again confronted with a difficulty, or at least a problem, which calls for explanation, in the fact that the vampire tradition and the records in support of it hail in such a preponderant degree from the Slavonic world. Why, it may be asked, should we not meet with the same phenomenon with the same frequency elsewhere? We do indeed meet with it occasionally, even as far back as in the records of Chaldea and Assyria, and the Romans were familiar with it, for the word *lamia* in the Latin dictionary admittedly corresponds to the modern English vampire. Perhaps the part of the world where such phenomena are least heard of or met with is India, and it is a remarkable fact in this connection, that the custom of cremation here is very general, and all vampire lore is agreed in asserting that the destruction of the body by fire is an effectual preventive of the dangers alleged to be consequent on the roaming of the living-dead in search of their prey. To drive a stake through the body of a vampire has been generally held to be sufficient to stop these predatory excursions, but cases are cited in which this has failed, and in which it was not until the body was actually consumed by fire that the trouble ceased.

The explanation of the phenomenon from the psychic point of view is given, by the celebrated French spiritualist, Pierart, who flourished about the middle of the last century, as follows :

"As long as the astral form is not entirely liberated from the body there is a liability that it may be forced by magnetic attraction to re-enter it. Sometimes it will be only half-way out when the corpse, which presents the appearance of death, is buried. In such cases the terrified astral soul re-enters its casket, and then one of two things happens: the person buried either writhes in the agony of suffocation, or, if he has been grossly material, becomes a vampire. The bi-corporeal life then begins. The ethereal form can go where it pleases, and as long as it does not break the link connecting it with the body can wander visible or invisible and feed on its victims. It then transmits the results of the suction by some mysterious invisible cord of connection to the body, thus aiding it to perpetuate the state of catalepsy."

The vampire, in the legendary records with regard to it, usually takes physical form, and it may be asked how it is possible for this to be transmitted from the grave to the outer air. This involves presumably an admission of the possibility of the disintegration and reintegration of the physical body. Can we look to the phenomena observed in connection with ectoplasm as an adequate explanation of this? It is noteworthy in any case that a number of records state that where vampirism had taken place there were discovered in the grave two or three holes about the size of a man's finger, penetrating beneath the soil, and it was argued that where these were to be found a body with all the marks of vampirism would be discovered within the grave. It is assumed that it is through these apertures that the fluidic body of the vampire escapes from the tomb. It is stated in all the records that when the grave of a vampire is opened the body is found wholly without decay, and as fresh and rosy as it had been in life. In one case, at a village called Kisolva, in Lower Hungary, a certain Peter Plogojovitz appeared after he had been buried ten weeks, and is stated to have killed nine persons within eight days. The inhabitants threatened to leave the village unless the corpse was dug up and burned. Accordingly the Commandant at Gradisca went with a priest from the same town and had the grave opened. The body was found entire and undecayed. The hair and beard had grown, and the old nails had fallen off and new ones come in their place. Quite fresh blood was found in the mouth, and when a stake was driven through the breast fresh blood poured forth from the wound, and also from the mouth and nose. This was in 1720, and a report of the case was sent to the Emperor. After this the body was cremated, and thenceforward the village was left in peace.

The following record was given by Dr. Franz Hartmann, and relates to a youth hired by a miller to labour in his mill. The story was told to Dr. Hartmann by a relative who was living at the mill in question when the occurrence took place. The youth hired by the miller was healthy and strong when first engaged, but by and by he began to look pale and emaciated, and his strength grew less from day to day. The miller inquired about his health, and eventually the boy confessed to him that every night towards midnight something heavy in the shape of a large-sized egg pressed upon his breast, causing a distressing nightmare and rendering him unable to breathe or move. In consequence of this confession the miller agreed to watch by the bedside of the boy, and made him promise to give a signal when he felt the presence of the vampire. On the night in question, while the miller was watching beside his bed, the boy gave the sign arranged, and the miller, putting out his hands, grasped the egg-shaped thing, which, although invisible to him, felt to his touch as if it were made of gelatine. He thereupon carried it to the chimney and threw it into the fire, after which the boy was no more troubled. The description given here is certainly very suggestive of ectoplasmic substance, and it will be noted that the incident is a comparatively recent one. It may be doubted, indeed, in spite of the lack of records, whether vampirism in one form or another is quite as absent from the conditions of modern civilisation as is commonly supposed. Although we are not today familiar with the Slavonic type of vampire that sucks the blood of its victims, producing death in two or three days' time, strange cases come to light occasionally where people are the victims, by their own confession, of something of a very similar nature, the vampire in these cases being an entity in human form who indulges in intercourse with someone of the opposite sex. Such cases are today, generally speaking, promptly consigned to one of our lunatic asylums and do not reach the public ear. I happened, however, quite recently to hear of an instance of the kind. The victim had been engaged to a young man, the family, on account of the man's antecedents, not approving of the engagement, but not being actively hostile. The man died suddenly, and the girl was prostrated with grief. Shortly after, however, she recovered her normal cheerfulness, and somewhat later confessed to her mother that she was visited by her former lover in physical form. She subsequently became engaged to another man, but owing to threats, as she said, of her deceased lover, the engagement was broken off. The last time I heard of the young lady in question she was stated to be consumptive. Naturally, these things do not get into the papers, and obviously the ordinary medical man will put down instances of the kind as pure hallucination. Still, if we have any belief in the philosophy of the occultist, they are bound to give us pause, and make us hesitate before saying that vampirism is entirely a thing of the past.

Some curious phenomena in connection with ectoplasmic emanations are recorded by Miss Scatcherd in a symposium recently published by Messrs. G.P. Putnam's and Sons, entitled *Survival*.[2] Miss Scatcherd gives certain of her own experiences, which suggest the partial re-materialisation of the dead by the utilisation of the material substance of the living.

> I saw ectoplasm [she says] in solid form for the first time when looking for rooms in the neighbourhood of Russell Square. My friend, many years older than myself, was tired. She wore a black velvet cloak, and was sitting on a high chair, so that her mantle hung in long folds to the ground, while the light from the large windows fell full on her face. Suddenly I observed, on her left side, just above the waist, a patch of cloudy white substance, becoming bigger and denser as I watched its uncanny growth. Meanwhile, I was discussing terms with the landlady, a frail little woman, when a look of terror came into her eyes. She, too, was staring transfixed at the globular mass of white substance on my companion's black mantle. For out of it looked a living face, normal in size - a man's face with rolling eyes and a leering grin that made one's blood run cold. When I mentally ordered him away, he grinned defiance. Fearing to startle my friend, I took the landlady aside and asked what was the matter. She burst into tears.
>
> "Oh, miss! did you not see him? He was my first. He's come like this several times, and has never forgiven me for marrying again."
>
> "What do you mean?" I asked again, very severely.
>
> "Oh!" she wailed. "You must have seen his wicked face glaring at us from your friend's cloak, and now you will not take the rooms!"

Such things can obviously only be possible where the person in question has the natural qualifications of a materialising medium, even though he or she may be quite unaware of these natural powers. Needless to say, the ordinary public will receive records of this kind with entire scepticism. I think it must be admitted that whether or not vampirism is an exploded superstition, it is in fact no more incredible than the phenomena of the materialising séance where physical forms are built up and disintegrated again in a few minutes of time. It may be contended that the phenomena of vampirism argue a certain knowledge of black magic on the part of the vampire, and to the absence of this at the present time may be attributed the rarity of such incidents. If, it may be argued, the deceased person has no knowledge of possibilities of the kind while on earth, it is unlikely that he will acquire it during the early part of his sojourn on the other side. After this, it is to be presumed, the possibility of such misuse of the physical body will have passed away.

An account is given by Miss Middleton, in her *Another Grey Ghost Book*[3], of a French viscount who survived the Revolution and became a vampire after his death, in order to get level with the friends of the new order of things. When the revolutionary movement had ebbed out, he took advantage of the disturbed state of the country to make away with his old retainers and workpeople one by one. Such drastic measures could not fail to meet with reprisal, and he himself in due course met his death by assassination at the hands of the peasantry. Not long after the viscount was laid in his grave an appalling number of young children died in the neighbourhood, all of these bearing the marks of vampirism on their throats. The existence of vampirism was not admitted by the French authorities, and nothing was done in the matter. Rumour, however, was busy, and it was said that, at a later date, while the tomb was being repaired nine more cases occurred in a single week. These stories reached the ears of the grandson of the original viscount, who consulted a priest with a view to laying his ancestor's ghost, and it was decided to open the tomb. On this being done, every coffin in the vault was found to have rotted away except that of the old viscount, which, after seventy-two years, was perfectly sound and strong. The lid was then removed and the body found fresh and free from decomposition. The face was flushed and there was blood in the heart and chest, the skin also being soft and natural. The body was thereupon removed from the coffin and a whitethorn driven through the heart of the corpse, with the result that blood and water gushed forth, and the corpse groaned and screamed. After this the remains were burned, whereupon the epidemic of infant mortality ceased.

This, like other records of the kind, makes a very serious demand on the credulity of the reader. To be asked to believe that a corpse which had been buried upwards of seventy years could have groaned and screamed is, it must be admitted, a tall order! And the trouble is that in the case of a number of these vampire stories confirmatory evidence is lacking. They impress us rather by their multiplicity and similarity than by the convincing character of any particular narrative, and we are naturally frequently suspicious that we are in the region of romance rather than actual fact. In any case it is probably necessary to allow a pretty generous margin for imaginative detail.

I have referred to the phenomena of ectoplasm and the materialising séance in connection with vampires. These clearly have a bearing on the matter; but in neither case do we find any parallel to the escape of a body that has been enclosed in a tomb, and we may ask ourselves whether, if there is any truth in vampirism, the body actually dematerialises and then reintegrates outside the tomb, or whether another body is built up by the vampire independently of the body which remains behind in the grave. If the latter is the case, we must assume that the body in question is built up by the methods adopted at a materialising séance, i.e. with the aid of a medium or mediums. There is a third hypothesis. We may assume that in the case of vampirism the etheric body of the vampire remains intact and that he withdraws ectoplasmic material from his own body in the tomb, which enables him to build up a physical form externally with further aid from the person or persons whom he vampirizes. This perhaps seems the most plausible hypothesis of the three.

Some further light is shed on this matter by what is perhaps the most extraordinary record of all in this connection, the account given of the visits of the Greek lady, Philinnion, to her lover, Machates. The date of this story, the fourth century B.C., some time during the reign of Philip II of Macedon, the father of Alexander the Great, might not unnaturally give rise to scepticism; but the record is very full and detailed, the incident having caused a great sensation at the time, and a report of it was sent by Hipparchus, a resident and possibly an official, at Amphipolis, in Macedonia, the city in which the incident occurred, to Arrhidaeus, a son of king Philip and half-brother to Alexander the Great. The parents were in a good social position, and Philinnion, their daughter, who was in love with Machates, was compelled against her will to marry Craterus, who subsequently became one of Alexander the Great's generals. Philinnion died, apparently broken-hearted, six months after the marriage. The incidents narrated took place another six months later. Philinnion, according to the record, appeared in her physical form to Machates in his bedroom, and visited him on several successive nights. On one of these occasions Philinnion's old nurse noticed a lamp in the room and recognised Philinnion, who was sitting on the bedside, and told the parents. The mother was sceptical, but eventually took Machates to task on the matter. He admitted the truth of what was said, but evidently had not believed that his lover was dead. In order to confirm the story he showed a gold ring which Philinnion had given him, and which apparently had been buried with her in her tomb, and also a belt which she had left behind. The parents, having now been informed of the state of the case, arranged to come and see their daughter the following night. They, too, could not believe that she was dead and threw themselves upon her with cries of joy. Philinnion, however, reproached them, exclaiming, "Father and Mother, cruel indeed have ye been in that ye grudged my living with the stranger for three days in my father's house, for it brought harm to no one. But ye shall pay for your meddling with sorrow. I must return to the place appointed for me, though I came not hither without the will of Heaven." After speaking thus she fell dead and her body lay stretched upon the bed. In consequence of the sensation caused by this incident the family vault was opened. On examination it was seen that the other bodies were lying as they had been placed at their burial, but on the bier where Philinnion's body had lain was found only the iron ring which had belonged to her lover, and the gilt drinking cup that Machates had given to her on the first day of their meeting.

In this record we find that not only had the body of Philinnion actually left the tomb, but that she had transferred from it a gold ring which was presented to her lover, and had also taken back to the tomb an iron ring and a gilt drinking cup which Machates had given her. In the upshot, Machates committed suicide. Hipparchus, in concluding the story, writes to his correspondent: "If you think it right I should give the king (i.e. Philip) an account of all this, let me know, and I will send some of those who gave me the various details." The narrative is obviously of all the greater interest, in that relatives and friends of people of such great historical note as Philip and Alexander of Macedon are mixed up in it. It is clear, too, that the incident created a great sensation in the locality, for, as Hipparchus observes, "the whole event was of great importance, and absolutely past belief." It appears also that various propitiatory rites were performed, and the temples reconsecrated, so that the "pollution" might be removed from the neighbourhood. As for Philinnion, it was ordered that her body should be re-interred outside the boundaries of the city.

A full account of this remarkable case was given by me in the *Occult Review* for February, 1913. It can also be found in a book entitled *Greek and Roman Ghost Stories*, published by B.H. Blackwell, of Oxford. Mrs. Crowe, in her *Night Side of Nature*, tells the story, but very inaccurately, giving the wrong date, and referring it to the times of the Emperor Hadrian. It seems, in spite of the early date of this narrative, impossible to put it aside as pure romance, and if the details are to be accepted, we have here a case of a girl who would, according to modern nomenclature, be described as a vampire, actually leaving her tomb in physical form. In her case, at least, if we may accept the narrative, complete disintegration and reintegration of the body must have taken place. We are bound also to ask, must it not also have taken place in the case of the drinking cup, which could hardly have otherwise been transferred to the vault? One may question, however, as this appears so very incredible, whether by any possibility the living-dead Philinnion might not have found some normal means of egress from the tomb. There is no recorded evidence to show whether or not the vault appeared to have been tampered with. Some who may be prepared to accept this extraordinary story at its face value will doubtless prefer to adopt this hypothesis. One hesitates to accept any record of so strange and startling a character as this; but it is hard to suppose that Hipparchus would have written a fairy story of such an incredible kind to his friend, the King's son, and we have also to take into account the opening of the tomb, which must have been a matter of common knowledge, no less than the purification of the temples. It must, it seems, be admitted that our knowledge of biology is still so slight that the dividing line between the possible and the impossible even now, in this twentieth century, eludes us at every turn.

1. Quoted in *Vampires and Vampirism*. By Dudley Wright. Second and enlarged edition. William Rider and Son, Ltd., 8 Paternoster Row, London, E.C.4. 5s. net.

2. *Survival*. By Various Authors. Edited by Sir James Marchant, K.B.E., LL.D. Putnams, London and New York. 7s. 6d. net.

3. London : Eveleigh Nash.

2. THE GHOSTLY TALE
– MUST THE AUTHOR BELIEVE?

~ Albert Power ~

Must the author of the ghost story believe in ghosts ? The powerful expression of the vampire legend in Bram Stoker's *Dracula* inevitably raises this lively question, and makes one wonder to what extent Bram Stoker and other writers of the supernatural actually believed in the world of spirits. It is difficult to offer a definitive answer.

Montague Summers (1880-1948), the renowned Gothic academician and anthologist, in the opening paragraph of his introduction to *The Supernatural Omnibus* (1931), argued, by example, the absurdity of such an assertion. A distinguished eighteenth century actor is performing in a period melodrama. Act One concludes with fine histrionics : "Who rules o'er freemen should himself be free." The audience is enraptured. All eyes turn towards Dr. Johnson, one of the guests, in expectation of some elegant congratulating quip. But Johnson, sternly facing the actor, is unimpressed. "Nay sir, "quoth he, "I cannot agree with you. It might as well be said : 'Who drives fat oxen should himself be fat.'"

An apt illustration of the tautology of the simple argument. But that is hardly the end of the matter. A little further on, Montague Summers makes a strong case for the need for inner conviction on the part of the writer of the spectral tale.

> "Can an author 'call spirits from the vasty deep' if he is very well satisfied that there are, in fact, no spirits to obey his conjurations? I grant that by some literary tour de force he may succeed in duping his readers, but not for long. Presently his wand will snap short, his charms will lose their potency and mystic worth; he will soon have turned the last page of his grimoire [magic spell book]; he steps all involuntarily out of the circle, the glamour dissipates and the spell is broken."

This is stylish advocacy, but the proposition is too tightly defined and its accuracy as a result challengeable. The spectral tale is a more subtle art form than the mere dextrous delineation of darkness and mystery dependent for its force on the author's inner convictions. That application of style and skill, derisively accorded second place by Summers to the personal persuasion of the writer, is indisputably a *sine qua non* to the successful telling of the terror tale. The ghost story to succeed needs to be both convincing and convincingly told.

M.R. James (1862-1936), that undisputed master of the scholarly spectral tale peppered with tersely limned scene-setting, precise placing of detail and a carefully gauged escalation of suspense, was under no illusion as to the crucial importance of technical skill in the writing of ghostly tales: "The ghost story is, at its best, only a particular sort of short story, and is subject to the same broad rules as the whole mass of them." M.R. James's own attitude to the existence of ghosts is, perhaps consistently, ambivalent : "Do I believe in ghosts ? To which I answer that I am prepared to consider evidence and accept it if it satisfies me." Therein lies the essence of M.R. James's fictional ghost stories and the reason for their success : a keen attention to detail and atmosphere, with measured narrative pacing which gradually tightens the screw of suspense.

But, for all that, do they succeed in beguiling the reader ? L.T.C. Rolt (1910-1974), author of that excellent collection of industrial and railway-related supernatural tales, *Sleep No More* (1948), has his doubts :

> "If James has a fault it is that he betrays, in some not easily definable way, a kind of impish glee, a malicious delight in his ability to frighten his readers. With infinite relish he sets about the task of freezing our blood and performs it most efficiently, but we are aware that his own blood has never cooled and that he does not believe a word of what he writes. If he is to carry his readers with him and achieve the highest pinnacle of success the writer of ghost stories must create the impression, whether it be true or false, that he himself believes that the events which he is describing could happen. If he does not do so he cannot hope to suspend his readers' disbelief."

A generation after M.R. James, the vivid and skilfully constructed supernatural tales of H.R. Wakefield (1888-1964) led to his being hailed on his death as the "undisputed dean of ghost story writers". Like M.R. James, the ghost stories of H.R. Wakefield are distinguished by masterful construction, stylish writing, carefully created atmosphere and a grim dénouement. Wakefield's tales stand apart from James's by dint of avoiding for the most part the restraints of the academic milieu and not being coy about themes like sexual obsession and the squalid brutality of inter-personal power play. Not surprisingly, Wakefield was rather more frank in his views on the reality of the supernatural.

In the introduction to his fourth collection of original ghost stories *The Clock Strikes Twelve* (1940), he wrote :

"We see perhaps only one octave of the rays of reality, and ghosts, it may be, lie outside that octave, or rather just in and just out of it; they are Dwellers on the Threshold. The realm in which they have their being lies just outside our area of comprehension, but not absolutely and at all times. . ."

It is perhaps significant that H.R. Wakefield's first ever ghost story, *The Red Lodge*, about the misfortunes of a family holidaying in a quaint country house that turns out to be haunted by half-seen patches of green slime of murderous inclination, was based on a real Queen Anne-period house with a long troubled reputation, in which Wakefield himself years earlier had had an uncanny experience.

One could perhaps, lawyer-like, continue from author to author, citing from their occasional dicta on the subjects of ghosts and ghost stories, piling up arguments, now on one side and now on the other. Absolute conviction in the actual existence of the supernatural is probably too demanding a test for the author of weird fiction. Even so, there is a strong case for contending that such a writer either must feel himself driven or must empathise with the likelihood of a different state of being. Notwithstanding this, in his remarkable essay on the evolution and current state of the terror tale, *Supernatural Horror in Literature* (1927), H.P. Lovecraft (1890-1937) observed that the true believer in the occult was probably less effective than the sceptic in the delineation of otherworldly atmosphere and spectral interference, precisely because the prospect of the return of the dead for such writers conforms with the natural order rather than representing a violation of it. Lovecraft himself, despite being a professed non-believer, could hardly have penned his Cthulhoid tales of ancient eldritch otherworldly beings routed from their ascendancy on this planet endless millennia in the past, striving to resume their coveted stranglehold, without having some conviction of the hidden awfulness which lurks beyond the boring borders of the normal. It is, in fact, Lovecraft's power, partly through the intensity of his vision, and partly through his elegant and ominous prose, to draw the reader beneath the mantle of his spectral tales and enfold him in that cobwebby winding sheet which is the story he is telling. Lovecraft's was a deep and complex inner world tightly bound up in a labyrinth of inhibitions. His writing style would not have been out of place in the eighteenth century (a fact on which he prided himself), and he never troubled to seek publication outside the pulp periodicals of his time. For all that, he succeeded well in satisfying his own declared test of supernatural effectiveness :

> "The one test of the really weird is simply this - whether or not there be excited in the reader a profound sense of dread, and of contact with unknown spheres and powers; a subtle attitude of awed listening, as if for the beating of black wings or the scratching of outside shapes and entities on the known universe's utmost rim."

This power to convince of the reality of otherworldly incursion often derives from the writer's personality, most noticeably if that personality is troubled or guilt-ridden, and in some cases from the writer's experience. Frequently a combination of both personality and experience provides the root for the most nightmarish literary efflorescence. It is a commonly recounted fact that Mary Shelley's *Frankenstein* (1818) was prompted by a grotesque dream following a discussion among her colleagues of the scientific possibilities of re-animation of dead tissue through galvanism. The fact that Mary was then living in an adulterous relationship with the poet Shelley, among a group of extravagant eccentrics at the Villa Diodati on the shores of Lake Geneva, may itself help to account for the themes of betrayal, shame and rejection which underlie the external trappings of this enduring Gothic novel.

In her specially composed introduction to *Frankenstein*, written thirteen years after the novel's first publication, Mary Shelley described the undeniable link between personal experience, however shadowy or subjective, and the writing of a tale of terror :

> "Invention, it must be humbly admitted, does not consist in creating out of void, but out of chaos; the materials must, in the first place, be afforded : it can give form to dark, shapeless substances but cannot bring into being the substance itself. . . . Invention consists in the capacity of seizing on the capabilities of a subject and in the power of moulding and fashioning ideas suggested to it."

In 1994 the Ghost Story Press brought out, in a sumptuous limited issue reprint edition, the rare collection of terror tales *Tales of the Grotesque* (1934) by the little remembered writer L.A. Lewis (1899-1961). Lewis presents virtually a case-book example of an author both whose own experiences and personal neuroses are amply reflected in his writings. The stories in *Tales of the Grotesque* evoke genuine unease and frequently stray to the more grotesque extremes of the Gothic genre's palette of dark hues.

Probably the best known story, by reason of its inclusion in other anthologies, is *The Tower of Moab*, the tale of a travelling salesman's discovery of a circular tower left incomplete in the centre of a town by an obscure religious sect that built it many years earlier. Booking into a dingy local hotel, the travelling salesman embarks on a heavy drinking binge. One night, filled to the gills with whiskey, he observes a ghostly extension from the top of the tower stretching right up as far as the eye can see. Inside the invisible funnel formed by this extension abounds a pantheon of otherworldly abominations. Unseen, except by the salesman in his liquor, they penetrate the human world, wreaking havoc and death wherever misery lurks.

Particularly unpleasant is Lewis's depiction of the wanton destruction of a stricken young girl on whom the invisible gargoyle demons descend. It is difficult to believe that this author was not writing from some profound and twisted inner conviction. The spirit of unspoken personal horror pervades the tense, tormented writing.

> "I was crouching, one vivid afternoon, at my usual post, watching through the chink of the blind a veritable flock of ghoulish wraiths whirling about a young girl who stood on the kerb, wearing on her face a look of desperation that spoke of private tragedy. All the bitterness of some shocking disillusionment was in that look. . . . all the while the spirit creatures whirled faster about - beckoning."

> "I was callously wondering what they wanted of her when the end came. She uttered a ghastly, sobbing scream, and hurled herself with a kind of boneless wriggle under the wheels of a lorry."

> "I swung round, startled at a chorus of low-pitched, but intensely dreadful, laugher from behind me."

The 1994 edition is prefaced by a fascinating introductory essay by anthologist and researcher Richard Dalby, titled *The Quest for Lewis*, in which he details his sleuth-like research into the life and writings of this elusive author. It is perhaps not surprising to learn from this that *The Tower of Moab* was based on an actual incomplete tower constructed by a religious sect which Lewis had once seen on the outskirts of London. Nor does it strike one as unusual, in light of his literary output, that Lewis suffered from hallucinations and depression for much of his life and had an abiding belief in the reality of the otherworldly. An unique aspect of

Lewis's conviction is the fact that seemingly he believed that aircraft have souls. During the First World War he had fought in the Royal Flying Corps, but was later invalided out. Both his experience in the war and his strange conviction about aircraft having souls are powerfully brought into play in two of the stories in *Tales of the Grotesque: Haunted Air* features a revolting aerial gremlin that ogles and intimidates pilots who fly over a particular tract of land causing mysterious suicide crashes and passengers jumping to their deaths; *The Iron Swine* concerns the nasty activities of an ugly-featured aeroplane which macabrely wreaks the deaths of its various pilots. There is a verisimilitude in these tales that goes beyond mere artistry or technique. Cleverness alone could not make them work so well.

Occasionally the provenance of supernatural inspiration is not a disturbed or driven personality, but a deep inner consciousness of the reality of spiritual powers. Canon J.S. Leatherbarrow (1908-1989), who spent most of his Church of England ministry in Worcestershire, demonstrates the propinquity of the otherworldly in his privately published collection *A Natural Body and a Spiritual Body* (1983). Set in the fictional parishes of Rudmet and Eastlea, and focusing on the vicissitudes of the Rudgement family, these short, affectionately told stories drift from past to present, backwards and forwards, touching one moment on the ghostly world and then back to our own, with a calm, gentle assurance that loses not a whit of its plausibility through the seeming ease with which it is achieved.

In his brief introduction, speaking of the origin of the stories, Leatherbarrow wrote :

> "I have sometimes been asked "Are they true"? I can only reply that they are
> partly autobiography, partly local history and partly sheer invention; and for the life
> of me I can't tell exactly where one category ends and the next begins."

Leatherbarrow's anthology was dedicated to the well-known author and film purchaser, Leslie Halliwell (1929-1989), who, with world-renowned eponymous tomes like *Halliwell's Filmgoer's Companion* and *Halliwell's Film Guide* behind him, himself turned to ghost story writing the same year with *The Ghost of Sherlock Holmes - Seventeen Supernatural Stories* (1984). This collection in its turn was dedicated to Leatherbarrow. Two more collections, *A Demon Close Behind* (1987) and *A Demon on the Stair* (1988), followed. Halliwell's ghost stories, cast somewhat in the mould of E.F. Benson, are often sited in exotic foreign locales, and not infrequently owe much to Halliwell's own background in television and cinema.

On the question of the existence of the supernatural, Halliwell wrote in his introduction to *A Demon Close Behind* (1987) :

"Do I believe in ghosts ? I think I saw one once, but that was more than forty years ago, oddly enough in the eighteenth century rectory then presided over by Stanley Leatherbarrow, who not only introduced me to the works of M.R. James but himself became no mean writer of supernatural tales and helped to inspire these further attempts by his old friend and pupil."

The dividing line between palpable faith in the otherworldly and evangelical zeal decked out in the raiment of supernatural fiction can be difficult to define. One writer who strayed to the outer limits of this boundary - and, in the view of some, even transgressed it - was the late Russell Kirk (1918-1994). For Kirk ghost stories were a modern allegory of the fight between good and evil, their purpose to convey through supernatural narrative the Christian message to a jaded and decadent world. But the story was always more than just a preacher's parable. In the introduction to his first collection, *The Surly Sullen Bell* (1962), Kirk stated:

"If I am asked whether I have ever perceived a ghost - why, I would be a poor creature if I hadn't, considering the places where I have gone and the stock from which I come. But the True Narration of this sort rarely succeeds as a work of literary art : it is too fragmentary and inconclusive."

The tales themselves assert Kirk's entitlement to a high place among the ranks of Gothic writers, while his faith in the after life and its immanence is manifest. A fine example is one of his later stories, *There's A Long, Long Trail A-Winding*, which won a World Fantasy Award, and appeared in his collection *The Princess of All Lands* (1979). This poignant tale of a weary down-and-out, who dies from exposure in an empty house haunted by the ghosts of its previous owners who had died tragically, shows a sensitivity of touch and a tenderness for the fate of its characters that is not typical nowadays.

In an essay, *A Cautionary Note on the Ghostly Tale*, appended to *The Surly Sullen Bell*, Russell Kirk urged that the author of ghostly tales ought to be imbued with a consciousness of the nearness of that other world he describes. "For the sake of his art, the author of ghostly narrations ought never to enjoy freedom from fear." In the very next sentence he adduces the example of the true Master of the ghost story, Joseph Sheridan Le Fanu (1814-1873), who, he states, literally died of fright. This assertion stems from a popular myth, often repeated, that Le Fanu based his later creepy tales on his nightmares, a recurrent one of which was that he stood in a large house which was about to fall down on him. On 7th February 1873, Le Fanu was found dead in his bed, his face rigid with terror. His doctor, who had known of the recurring dream, pronouncing him dead, added, "I feared this - that house fell at last."

Whether there be truth in this story, or not, there can be no doubt that Le Fanu is a classic example of the connection between a writer's outpourings and the secret world of his personality and convictions. Unlike the other authors referred to, Le Fanu is not known to have written of his views on the supernatural. Yet, that the outer world of dark and sinister stirrings troubled him, there can be no dispute.

The Dublin-born son of a Church of Ireland clergyman, who married the daughter of a Munster Circuit barrister, and lived most of his life in his father-in-law's Dublin house at Merrion Square, the external details of Le Fanu's life disclose little cause for his fascination with ghostly fiction. Yet, even to dig slightly beneath the surface is to unearth much that is disquieting and awry : his failure to make a living at the bar despite his father-in-law's pre-eminence and that of several of his college friends, such as William Keogh and John Walsh who became judges; his lack-lustre enthusiasm for religion despite growing up in the glebe house; the obsessive paranoia and death-fixation of his young wife; her own premature death and his resultant reclusion from society; his strange practice of writing his ghost stories propped up in bed during the small hours, sustained by a diet of strong tea. Against such a background it is small wonder that the ghost stories of Joseph Sheridan Le Fanu are of that insidious, subtly hair-raising kind in which the normal becomes gradually and inexorably abnormal and the supernatural persecution can almost, but not quite, be explained away as the tugging of a troubled conscience.

In *The Watcher*, that nasty, squat little man who dogs with such unpredictable persistence the footsteps of Captain Barton, driving him first to breakdown and finally to death, may or may not be the ghost of the sailor who died of his injuries following a flogging at sea while under Barton's command; but if he is a mere figment of fancy, how explain the indentations on Barton's bed beside the dead body of Barton crouched up against the head of the bed, his features frozen with fright ? *In Squire Toby's Will*, the ugly white dog which writhes in obscene ecstasy on a grave in the churchyard may or may not be the supernatural incarnation of the dead squire, troubled at having disinherited his elder son in favour of the younger, while a deed of entail in the elder son's favour languished in a closet in an upstairs room; but if there is nothing more to it than a mere mangy mongrel, why does it haunt the young squire in his dreams, and who are the two black mantled strangers who arrive at the door after the elder son's funeral, enter without invitation and are never seen to leave ? And why from that day forth are the domestics troubled by unseen noises and threatening voices ? And why does young Squire Charles hang himself at the last in that very closet of the very room where the deed of entail had been hidden ?

The disturbing supernatural tales of Joseph Sheridan Le Fanu are surely inspired by more than the mere desire to frighten. In the subtly atmospheric unfolding of plot, bit by bit making the natural unnatural, and the gradual accumulation of disquieting detail, we see the tortured operation of a mind not at rest which feels no great surprise at incursion from the outer realms.

Then there are those authors who, though their writings are fictional, demonstrate clear conviction in forces beyond the ordinary and are driven by that conviction. In the constraints of an essay such as the present the many ghostly effusions of Arthur Machen (1863-1947) and Algernon Blackwood (1869-1951) can receive but scant attention. But the terror tales of these authors largely make the case themselves. They are imbued with an earnestness about the otherworldly that does not try to hide itself.

Machen's tales demonstrate the melancholy of the disenchanted loner steeped in the memory of the rolling hills, beneath which ancient gnome-like entities lurk, of his beloved native Wales. Blackwood's many stories evoke the awe-stirring majesty of the pitiless world of nature. The limitless expanse and overwhelming vastness of the Canadian forests are a typical theme with Blackwood, best embodied in that haunting long story of the unseen wind demon, *The Wendigo*, which steals through the door of his tent an unwary forest traveller asleep in his camp bed, and drags him at lightning speed over the unending terrain, until the feet are burnt off him and he becomes one as the Wendigo itself. I well remember first reading this tale as a boy of twelve and spending an uneasy night, because there was a window opposite the foot of my bed, and I was scared lest something should creep in and steal me away to some unknown wilderness where I had no wish to go.

We do not know for certain whether Bram Stoker harboured any belief in the supernatural. He is not known to have written on the subject, though the strenuous demands of his work with Henry Irving hardly make this surprising. Yet given his background - his bed-ridden years as a child, his mother's stories of the cholera epidemic in Sligo, his friendship with the Wildes - and the frequency with which he turned again and again to the Gothic theme in his writings, it is hard to conclude but that Bram Stoker too was aware that there was more than mere clever invention to the macabre fantasies which made him, so belatedly, famous.

The ghost story as an art form weaves a dark and lingering enchantment. At its most consummate there is no better entertainment. Yet it is a challenging type, which demands both high competence and sure conviction. Without true artistic skill, mastery of expression and a sensitivity to atmosphere and pace, the would-be writer in this genre cannot hope to succeed. The ghostly tale well told is a supreme achievement. But to succeed in veracious effect, as to succeed at all it must, the author of the ghostly tale yet needs to evince belief, attested in the tale itself, that such strange things may be, or, better still, are.

3. The Story of Dracula

Bram Stoker's *Dracula* is one of the most widely read and influential books of the past century. If you happen to be one of the few people who have never read the book or seen one of the various films about it, here is a brief outline of what it is all about:

Dracula is a vampire – an individual who lives on the blood of victims, biting their throats with his fang-like teeth. A vampire does not die, but after apparent death and burial, rises from his coffin to continue preying on living victims. If the victims die through loss of blood, they in turn become vampires. The 'undead' vampire sleeps in his coffin during daytime, rising at night to prey on his victims. He has supernatural powers and sometimes changes his shape to that of a werewolf. He may appear like a normal human being, but his undead character is evident by the fact that he casts no reflection in mirrors. He is usually repelled by making the sign of the cross, or by protecting oneself with the herb garlic. He is finally laid to rest by either driving a stake through his heart, or cutting off his head and burning the body. Women, as well as men, may become vampires.

The story opens with the English solicitor, Jonathan Harker, journeying through the ghostly landscape of Transylvania to the grim castle of Count Dracula, who wishes to purchase an estate in England. Harker is engaged to Mina Murray.

During a terrifying time at the castle, Harker discovers that the Count is a vampire, who attacks him. The Count consigns boxes of earth to the property in England which Harker has negotiated. A vampire likes to rest in his native soil. The Count himself makes his way to England, leaving Harker imprisoned. Although victimised by the vampire, Harker escapes from the castle. On his way home through Budapest, he is tended at a hospital, where the sisters write to inform Mina of his arrival.

Mina has been staying with her friend Lucy at Whitby, a harbour town on the North Yorkshire coast. Lucy has been suffering from ill health. She has three admirers – Quincey P. Morris from Texas, Dr. John Seward, doctor at a mental hospital, and Arthur Holmwood, to whom Lucy becomes engaged. All three men were old friends who had been together in Korea. Seward has a strange mad patient named Renfield, who at first appears to be fond of small creatures.

Meanwhile the vampire Count with his boxes of Transylvanian soil, is on his way to England on the ship *Demeter*. In England, Dr. Seward's patient Renfield becomes excited, babbling that "the Master is coming!" Seward at first interprets this as religious mania. In a severe storm, the *Demeter* is beached on the Whitby coast. About this time, Lucy walks in her sleep, and when Mina finds her, she sees something black bending over her. There are two small marks on Lucy's neck. Although tired and listless, she seems to get better for a time, and now Mina, who has heard that Jonathan is in the Budapest hospital, travels there to see him. When his health improves, they get married.

Back in England, Lucy returns to London, where she is joined by Arthur Holmwood, who asks Dr. Seward to examine Lucy. Puzzled by her condition, Seward consults his Dutch friend, Abraham Van Helsing, who has special knowledge of unusual diseases. Van Helsing prescribes blood transfusion. Both Holmwood and Seward donate their blood. Without further explanation, Van Helsing puts a garland of garlic around Lucy's neck, but unfortunately this is carelessly removed, resulting in another vampire attack. Meanwhile Jonathan and Mina have returned to England, alarmed at Lucy's worsening condition. Quincey Morris volunteers to give a blood transfusion to Lucy, but by now it is too late. Lucy dies and is buried in the family vault.

Soon there are reports of a lady attacking children during the night, and it is clear that Lucy herself has become a vampire. Van Helsing explains the dangers and precautions necessary in dealing with vampires. The men watch in the vault where Lucy's coffin is empty, and see her return with blood on her lips. After she returns to her coffin, Holmwood himself drives a stake through Lucy's heart. Van Helsing cuts off her head and fills her mouth with garlic. Lucy's fiendish expression vanishes and her face once again becomes sweet and pure as she expires in peace, released from the vampire curse.

Now the men combine forces to hunt out and destroy the master vampire, Dracula. In the asylum, Seward's patient Renfield is found to have been eating the small creatures that he desired, absorbing their vitality like a vampire. He attacks Seward who calls in Van Helsing to help him. Renfield reveals that Dracula is now attacking Mina, who has also suffered from tiredness and loss of energy. One night Dracula appears in Mina's bedroom and attacks her again, telling her that she will be "flesh of my flesh". Just in time the men rush in and save her.

They locate and destroy the earth coffins in London where Dracula lurks. Van Helsing hypnotises Mina, who discloses that Dracula has now left England on a ship, returning to Transylvania. Mina accompanies the men on their journey to Castle Dracula to finally destroy the vampire Count.

Because of the link between Mina and Dracula, Mini is the bait for Dracula, but is protected by Van Helsing's powerful ritual circle. There is a desperate encounter with a band of gypsies who are carrying the great chest containing Dracula lying in his Transylvanian soil. Just at the last moment, the sun sets, and Dracula rises from the chest and turns on Mina and the heroes, but is repelled and swiftly destroyed by both Jonathan Harker and Quincey Morris. Because Dracula was a 500 year old King Vampire his passing was different from that of his victim vampires. His body crumpled into dust. The world is freed from the evil monster.

But the legend of Dracula lives on, in other books, plays and special studies.

This brief summary gives only the bare bones of the story, omitting many fascinating details, and of course the powerful atmosphere generated by Stoker's writing, telling a complex story through the letters and journals of the main characters. This thrilling and terrifying story has become one of the world's classics.

__Dracula__ has been translated into many different languages and read all over the world. An Irish language translation by Seán Ó Cuirrín was published in Dublin in 1933 by Oifig Díolta Foillseacháin Rialtais. Many Irish people read the story for the first time in the Irish language.

Lovers of the Irish language will be glad to know that An Gúm (the Government Publications Office) is publishing a completely new Irish language translation, to celebrate the Centenary of Dracula.

4. THE WRITING OF DRACULA

~ Leslie Shepard ~

As a writer of fiction, Stoker had a strong tendency toward fantasy, horror and sensationalism. This is hardly surprising, since as a child he suffered from an illness that kept him weak and bedridden for some eight years of his early life, although surprisingly, he later recovered and became an athletic champion during his student days at Trinity College. We do not know what his illness was, or how he recovered so miraculously, but clearly his childhood was filled with unhappy dreams, intensified by his mother's weird stories of the Banshee, and a horrifying account of a cholera plague in Sligo in 1832, when some living victims were buried with the dead. It is not surprising that he should later write of the un-dead world of the vampires.

At Trinity College, where he became president of the Philosophical Society, he once delivered a paper on "Sensationalism in Fiction and Society". A lover of theatre, he would also have been strongly influenced by stage melodrama.

After leaving Trinity College and taking up a position as a civil servant at the Petty Sessions Office in Dublin Castle, he became an unpaid theatre critic for the Dublin *Evening Mail*, and also began to write short stories.

His first fiction was a story entitled *The Crystal Cup*. published in the magazine *London Society* in September 1872. The style is feverishly overblown, with little action but much extravagant musing on life and death and the plight of a captive in a palace dungeon, perhaps influenced by his childhood confinement through illness. Lines like "Oh Death, grim King of Terrors, how mighty is thy sceptre!" hint at the morbid theme later explored in *Dracula*.

The Crystal Cup was followed by another horror story *The Chain of Destiny*, concerning an invalid in a ghostly house, haunted by 'The Phantom of the Fiend', but restored by the love of a pure woman. This story was serialised in *The Shamrock* magazine in 1875.

Meanwhile another Irish writer, Joseph Sheridan Le Fanu, had published *Carmilla*, a haunted Gothic story of a female vampire. Stoker read this story, and it must have remained in his mind in the years before he wrote his own vampire story *Dracula*.

Stoker's first fiction book *Under the Sunset* further developed the Gothic themes of death, disease and horror that preoccupied him. Two illustrations from that book clearly indicate motifs later developed in *Dracula*. The first is the giant phantom form of the dreaded plague

The Plague of Doom hanging over the city.
(A page from Stoker's *Under the Sunset,* 1881)

hovering over the doomed 'Country Under the Sunset'; the second is the grim castle of the King of Death. The former is vividly reminiscent of the scene of the giant plague of the Devil hovering over a doomed city in F. W. Murnau's classic silent film *Faust* (1926). It will be remembered that Murnau had earlier directed the famous pirated film version of *Dracula* titled *Nosferatu* in 1921. Perhaps Murnau had seen Stoker's book *Under the Sunset*. Another curious precursor is the choice of Transylvania as the locale in *Dracula*, where the earlier 'Country Under the Sunset' became 'The Land Beyond the Forest'.

Stoker himself once claimed whimsically that the idea of his story came from a nightmare after a large supper of dressed crab, when he dreamed of a vampire king arising from his tomb. But clearly the main Gothic themes and atmosphere were well established before Stoker met the intrepid traveller Arminius Vambéry who was an authority on the history and legends of Transylvania. Vambéry may have given Stoker the locale of Transylvania for his story, and also the name of Vlad Dracula, a tyrant of fifteenth century Wallachia. This is implied by the sentence in Stoker's book where his character Dr. Van Helsing says: "I have asked my friend Arminius of Buda-Pesth University, to make his record; and, from all the means that are, he tell me of what has been. He must, indeed, have been that Voivode [prince] Dracula who won his name against the Turk . . ." But Vlad Dracula was not a vampire, although in his bloodthirsty campaigns he suspended hundreds of victims on stakes and feasted among the dripping blood. Vambéry may have told Stoker enough about the superstitions and history of Transylvania to inspire further research.

Clive Leatherdale's valuable book *The Origins of Dracula* (1987) explores in detail the works that Stoker researched for his story. Amongst these were Dom Augustine Calmet's *The Phantom World*; or, *The Philosophy of Spirits and Apparitions* (2 vols., 1850, a translation of a work originally published in Paris in 1746), William Wilkinson's *An Account of the Principalities of Wallachia and Moldavia (1820)*, and Emily Gerard's essay *Transylvanian Superstitions* (*The Nineteenth Century* magazine, July 1885). Calmet's book has many accounts of vampires. These books, and a score of others, furnished Stoker with reliable background information on vampire superstitions, Transylvanian history and legends, and supernatural beliefs.

It is astonishing that Stoker managed to find time to write Dracula or the nine other novels, various other books and articles that he published.

Being Theatre Manager to actor Henry Irving was a full time job. Stoker took charge of the Lyceum Theatre finances, managed the manifold details of scenery and props, and organised the tours of the whole company, sometimes involving a whole trainload of people and theatrical gear on journeys as far afield as America. He wrote some fifty or sixty letters a day, many for Irving, who merely signed them, and others on his own account. He even advised members of the cast. He took charge of the day to day running of the theatre. His literary work had to be crammed into occasional holidays in between productions.

Stoker spent three weeks in the Yorkshire town of Whitby, which he later made the location for the shipwreck that brought Dracula to England. It was at Whitby, too, that he studied in the well stocked local library, where he consulted William Wilkinson's book on Wallachia and Moldavia, which not only provided authentic local colour used in *Dracula*, but explained that 'Dracula' also means 'Devil', a detail also emphasised in Emily Gerard's essay on Transylvania superstitions. Stoker was fascinated with the theme of the pact with the Devil in *Faust*, which had been one of Henry Irving's most impressive and successful productions in both Britain and America. Stoker had also studied the legends of *The Flying Dutchman*,

A page from *Stoker's Under the Sunset*, 1881

and *The Wandering Jew*.

He wrote his own book at the holiday location of Cruden Bay, Scotland, a wild and lonely fishing village between Aberdeen and Peterhead. He also made it the setting for his story *The Watter's Mou'*, published in 1895. He spent seven years researching, plotting and writing *Dracula*. His research notes, now preserved in the Rosenbach Foundation Library, Philadelphia, record the evolution of the plot over several years. The 85 pages of manuscript and typescript also indicate Stoker's passion for authentic backgrounds and accurate detail. There are notes on the different locations of Whitby and London, the geography of Transylvania, routes and train timetables, shipwrecks, medical details of injuries, burial customs, vampire superstitions, mesmerism and trance, and much else.

There are intriguing echoes of real life names of people and places. The name of the character Jonathan Harker derives from that of the scenery designer at the Lyceum Theatre. The name Westenra for the character Lucy derives from the Westenra family in County Monaghan. The name Lucy could have been from Stoker's friend Lucy Clifford, who called him 'Uncle Bram'. The estate of Carfax in Purfleet, purchased by Count Dracula, refers to a real Carfax Abbey. The Insane Asylum where Renfield is confined is clearly Colney Hatch, a name that became synonymous with insanity.

Stoker's notes show that in addition to a faithful depiction of Whitby, he also based the episode of the shipwreck of the *Demeter* on the real wreck of the *Dmitry*, a Russian schooner from Marva, which ran aground near Whitby in 1885.

There has been some speculation that Dracula's Castle may have been based on Slains Castle at Cruden Bay, but there were many castles that Stoker must have seen in his travels through Ireland as Inspector of Petty Sessions. Like the character of Dracula himself, the castle is a composite creation. The basic idea of a grim castle of death was established as early as Stoker's first fiction book *Under the Sunset*.

The character who gives the book its title was originally an 'old dead man made alive' before becoming the vampire Count. In the notes he acquires the name Count Wampyr - 'wampyr' being one of many European names for a vampire. A later correction substitutes the name 'Dracula', but the typescript of the book (acquired by a Californian book dealer) indicates that right up to the last minute the book was titled *The Un-Dead*, and was only changed to *Dracula* shortly before publication. A few days after

Title. (i page)

THE. UN-DEAD
By.
Bram Stoker.
author of " Under the
Sunset ", The Snake's Pass,
"The Watter's Mou ", The
Shoulder of Shasta ".

Copyright 1897 By
Bram Stoker. All Rights Reserved.

The original title page in Stoker's own handwriting.
The title was changed to *Dracula* shortly before printing.

publication, Stoker organised a reading of the book in rough play format, in order to protect copyright for stage performance. There was a printed Lyceum Theatre Programme which gave the Title *Dracula or The Un-Dead*. The performance was witnessed by only a handful of friends and the Lyceum staff and cleaners.

There has been much speculation about the character of Dracula. In the book, Stoker introduces him as a tall old man with a long white moustache, with protuberant sharp white teeth and bad breath. He has a strong aquiline face, with high bridge of his nose, arched nostrils, and a lofty domed forehead. He was clad in black. There is some resemblance to a woodcut illustration of the historic Vlad Dracula in a fifteenth century pamphlet which Stoker must have seen during his researches. It has been suggested that Stoker may have unconsciously modelled Dracula on the actor Henry Irving, who had strong aquiline features, a commanding, almost hypnotic presence, and who dominated Stoker's life for a quarter of a century. It may be possible, but seems unlikely. Stoker idolised Irving, and willingly and loyally devoted himself to the actor's success, and was heartbroken at his death.

The fifteenth century tyrant of Transylvania, Vlad Tepes (the Impaler)

Even more farfetched is the suggestion that the book itself is an allegory of the oppression of Ireland by foreign occupation, sucking vitality from a victimised country. Stoker was too absorbed in literature and theatre to have time for politics during his early life in Ireland and took no part in the question of Irish independence. In his single-minded attention to the theatre of Henry Irving, he became cosmopolitan in outlook.

There are two sections missing from Stoker's original manuscript. First, a complete chapter, in which there is a Walpurgis Night with a lone traveller and werewolves, featuring a tomb in Styria, clearly a reference to Le Fanu's *Carmilla*. This was excised from the published work presumably for reasons of length and continuity. An important paragraph at the end of the story was also excised; this described a cataclysmic convulsion in which the castle of Dracula is totally destroyed and swallowed up in the earth, somewhat in the style of the ending of Edgar Allen Poe's story *The Fall of the House of Usher*, which Stoker may have had in mind. But the book retains its extraordinary power even without this apocalyptic end scene.

The allegorical elements in the story spring from very deep roots. The age-old battle between god and evil, love and death, the morbid fears of blood and sickness (summarised in the Biblical text 'For the blood is the life'), the Gothic frissons of haunted castles, the decay of the body in graveyards, are all basic archetypal themes that have sustained the appeal of Stoker's book all over the world for a century, giving rise to so many other books, plays, movies and solemn academic studies.

Like all of Stoker's literary work, the book was written hastily, although its preparation involved complex and detailed research over six years. It has a passionate intensity lacking in some of his other stories. It is undoubtably a classic of Gothic fiction, and has created a mythology of its own.

Stoker himself always gave first place in his life to the work with Henry Irving in the theatre, but by now this has almost totally been eclipsed in popular memory by this book and the profound influence it has exercised. A modern world has forgotten Henry Irving, but everyone is familiar with the name Dracula.

Perhaps the last word should be with the author's mother. Charlotte Stoker wrote to her son: "My dear, it is splendid, a thousand miles beyond anything you have written before, and I feel certain will place you very high in the writers of the day . . ."

5. WHY WESTENRA?

~ Mark Pinkerton ~

Some years ago I bought a second hand book *Irish Church Monuments 1570-1880* by Homan Potterton (published by the Ulster Architectural Heritage Society, 1975). Leafing through it, I came across the photograph of a memorial bas-relief in Saint Patrick's Church of Ireland church in Monaghan : "The Parting Glance" - memorial to Lady Rossmore (1843) by Thomas Kirk. As can be seen from the illustration below, it depicts a woman on her deathbed with a male figure bending over her and another male figure holding him back.

I was forcibly reminded of the deathbed scene of Lucy Westenra in *Dracula* :

'And then insensibly there came the strange change which I had noticed in the night. Her breathing grew stertorous, the mouth opened and the pale gums, drawn back, made the teeth look longer and sharper than ever. In a sort of sleep-waking, vague, unconscious way she opened her eyes, which were now dull and hard at once, and said in a soft, voluptuous voice, such as I had never heard from her lips :-

"Arthur! Oh, my love, I am ever so glad you have come! Kiss me!" Arthur bent eagerly over to kiss her; but at that instant Van Helsing, who, like me, had been startled by her voice, swooped upon him, and catching him by the neck with both hands, dragged him back with a fury of strength which I never thought he could have possessed, and actually hurled him almost across the room.

"Not for your life! he said; "Not for your living soul and hers!"

Turning to the text of *Irish Church Monuments 1570-1880*, I read : 'Mary Anne Rossmore (died 1807) the first wife of Warner William Westenra, Baron Rossmore, is commemorated by a relief entitled "The Parting Glance". Lord Rossmore, restrained by his son, takes a last look at his deceased wife.'

Warner William Westenra! Westenra is not a common name. I have never come across any suggestion as to why Bram Stoker should have chosen this surname for Lucy. Is it possible that he might have seen this striking memorial and been influenced by it?

I have read - although I cannot recall where - that the novel *Dracula* had its seeds in a nightmare experienced by the sickly young Stoker resulting from the presence of nurses around his bed, which was transmogrified into the scene in the library of Castle Dracula where Jonathan Harker awakes surrounded by the three female vampires. Is it possible that the Westenra monument might have had a similar effect on an impressionable young mind?

I do not know if there is any record of Stoker having visited Monaghan. His mother's people came from Sligo, which is not that far away. Certainly Stoker was known for his interest in churches and memorials of the dead.

It is of interest, if not of relevance, that Christopher Frayling in his *Vampyres : Lord Byron to Count Dracula* refers to a tale of Lady Wilde [Oscar's mother] with which Stoker, as a friend of the Wildes, may have been familiar, about 'the demon bride who was said to haunt a churchyard in County Monaghan and to drain the vitality of passers by.'

According to Burke's Peerage, the original Warner Westenra settled in Ireland from Holland in the reign of Charles II. His grandson Henry married Harriet, daughter of Sir Alexander Cairns, of Monaghan. One of

Sir Alexander's older daughters, Elizabeth, married General the Right Honourable Robert Cunningham, who was created first Baron Rossmore in 1796. He died without issue and the title passed to Henry Westenra's son Warner William (of the memorial) who thus became second Baron. Warner William's first wife, Mary Anne, was the second daughter of Charles Walsh of Walsh Park, County Tipperary.

There are supernatural events associated with the Rossmore family : specifically with the first Baron, General Robert Cunningham. Sir Jonah Barrington, in his *Recollections*, records mysterious happenings attending the general's death in 1801. In August of that year the Barringtons were staying with the Rossmores at Mount Kennedy in County Wicklow. Sir Jonah was wakened at 2 a.m. on the 6th by a mysterious, plaintive sound which 'resembled neither a voice nor an instrument; it was softer than any voice and wilder than any music and seemed to float in the air.' The sound continued for half an hour and culminated with a 'deep, heavy, throbbing sigh . . . shortly succeeded by a sharp but low cry and by the distinct exclamation, thrice repeated, of "Rossmore, Rossmore, Rossmore"'. When the household arose that morning, Sir Jonah learnt that Lord Rossmore had suddenly and unexpectedly died during the night at just the time he had heard the mysterious voice. Tales of the cry of the banshee attending the death of members of prominent Irish families are, of course, numerous.

The Westenras played a prominent part in public life in Monaghan in the nineteenth century. Warner William was a supporter of Catholic emancipation. He contributed ten guineas towards the erection of a high altar in St. Mary's Catholic church in 1796 and his son, Henry Robert (who features on the monument) won the Monaghan seat in the 1826 parliamentary election as an advocate of Catholic emancipation with the support of Daniel O'Connell. According to Peadar Livingstone in *The Monaghan Story*: 'The Westenras controlled the Corporation of Monaghan until its demise in 1844.'

Later in the century, the Rossmores were active opponents of Home Rule and are even celebrated in a loyalist ballad; 'Lord Rossmore led his column/Past the rebels to Roslea . . . Cheers for gallant Rossmore/With Monaghan's brave men.'

The family seat, Rossmore Castle, was abandoned in the 1940s and demolished in the 1970s. The family continued to use a cottage in the Park

until it was burned down by republican sympathisers during the Maze Prison hunger strike of 1981.

I would be interested to hear from any readers who may know anything about possible connections between Stoker and Monaghan, or, indeed, may have alternative suggestions as to why the name Westenra was chosen for Lucy.

I am grateful to Mary Connolly for providing the line drawing of the Rossmore memorial.

6. THE GOTHIC NOVEL AND BRAM STOKER

~ Leslie Shepard ~

Leslie Shepard traces the origin of the term 'Gothic Novel' and discusses Bram
Stoker's *Dracula* in the context of this literary form, its continuing influence for
a century, and the need for Bram Stoker to be honoured in his own country.

G othic literature occupies a peculiar position midway between high
and low literature, between folklore and sophistication. It played a
considerable part in shaping the English novel, and its influence is
still very much alive today.

Three Irish writers played an important part in development of the
Gothic Novel. They were: Charles Robert Maturin (1780 - 1824), Joseph
Sheridan Le Fanu (1814 - 1873) and Bram Stoker (1847 - 1912). All three
were born in Dublin and educated at Trinity College, Dublin.

The Gothic Romance crystallized as a literary genre during the
eighteenth century with the famous story *The Castle of Otranto* by Horace
Walpole (1717 - 1797), aristocrat, wit and dilettante. Walpole's book, first
published 1764, was subtitled *A Gothic Story*. It was originally claimed to be
a translation from an old Italian Work printed in the old black-letter type
known as 'Gothic', but in the second edition Walpole dropped this
mystification and acknowledged himself as the sole author.

Walpole was obsessed with everything Gothic. In 1747, he had leased
the Strawberry Hill estate near Twickenham, where he spent a decade in
building what he called 'a little Gothic castle'. By 1760, the castle had a
round tower, gallery, cloisters, chapel, and was furnished with period
antiques. Walpole lived in a dream world of revival Gothic architecture
and mock medievalism. The story *The Castle of Otranto* was filled with the

architecture of Walpole's Strawberry Hill castle, and even the supernatural theme derived from a dream within in a dream, when he saw upon the uppermost banister of a great staircase a vision of a gigantic hand in armour.

In his preface to the second edition, Walpole explained that his story was 'an attempt to blend the two kinds of romance, the ancient and the modern' and create 'a new species of romance' through setting free 'the great resources of fancy . . . damned up by a strict adherence to common life.' In short, Walpole developed a literary form which was a reaction against realistic novels, combining fantasy, sentimentalism and supernatural elements in a setting of mock-medieval architecture.

This mixture launched a thousand imitations and variations, and had a lasting influence on the course of English Literature. After *Otranto* came such other key works as Clara Reeve's *The Old English Baron; A Gothic Story* in 1778 (originally published a year earlier under the title *The Champion of Virtue*), Mrs. Ann Radcliffe's *The Mysteries of Udolpho* (1794) and Matthew Gregory Lewis's staggeringly successful book *The Monk* (1796). Stock ingredients of the Gothic novel were such plot elements as pure young virgins and chivalrous heroes, embroiled with scoundrels of continental origin (usually Italians), dastardly monks, cruel inquisitors and ruthless bandits, in a setting of gloomy castles, ruined abbeys, dismal dungeons, bloodstained daggers, skulls, sliding panels, secret rooms, magic books, animated portraits – a twilight world of dark forests, pale moonlight and nameless terrors lurking behind the rocks. Some Gothic writers (like Clara Reeve) explained away apparently supernatural events; others (like Walpole) left them as unequivocably other-worldly.

Such 'horrid mysteries' (as Jane Austen called them in *Northanger Abbey*) became the mainstay of the rapidly developing circulating libraries in every large town and city, and the pop literature of their day, supplanting the penny broadsides of old balladry as urban tastes became sophisticated.

Curiously enough, it was ancient folklore that reinforced the Gothic revival, with the publication of Bishop Thomas Percy's *Reliques of Ancient English Balladry* only a couple of months after the appearance of Walpole's *Castle of Otranto*. Percy's work introduced polite society to traditional balladry, and gave a new impulse to European literature, culminating in the German romantic movement of Herder and Bürger, and in Britain, of Scott, Wordsworth, Coleridge, Burns and others. Soon it became possible for cultured gentlemen to collect folk music from uncultured peasants, while the most polished writers tried to copy the style of ancient balladry. Together Percy's *Reliques* and Walpoles *Otranto* launched the Gothic Revival in English Literature, a romantic preoccupation with an ancient past, with heroic legends, chivalry and ornate architecture. Other country gentlemen followed Walpole in remodelling their estates with mock castles, follies and grottoes. Some even employed old men to live as 'hermits' in artificially constructed caverns, in a kind of Gothic Disneyland.

There were, of course, continental parallels of the Gothic influence in German writers, and in the French *romans noir* (black romances) of François-Thomas de Baculard D'Arnaud, and not least in the horrific writings of the Marquis de Sade, whose horrendous books were undoubtedly Gothic in character, although minutely describing every conceivable sexual perversion and sado– masochism instead of hinting at vague horrors.

Scott's *Ivanhoe* and Waverley novels were a by–product of both Percy's *Reliques* and Walpole's *Castle of Oranto*, and the Gothic novel was a major influence on such poets as Shelley and Byron. The Gothic impulse was both the strength and weakness of such authors and poets. The genuine folklore roots of heroic balladry and chivalry were a firm foundation, but their adaption to the the elegant sophisticated literary setting of the eighteenth century led to artificiality at best, and mawkish sentimentality at worst. It is a mixture that has remained constant up to modern times.

The success of the Gothic novel amongst upper and middle classes was soon merchandised at a more popular level in abridged and pirated versions in cheap paper-covered pamphlets. The forerunners of today's paperback books sold at sixpence or a shilling each, and were known as 'bluebooks' (from the blue paper covers) or 'shilling shockers'. Many of them imitated the technique of the old chapbook penny pamphlets in giving extended titles and subtitles amounting to a complete plot synopsis, such as:

Lovel Castle, or the Rightful Heir restored, a Gothic Tale; Narrating how a Young Man, the Supposed Son of a Peasant, by a Train of Unparalleled Circumstances, not only Discovers who were his Real Parents, but that they came to Untimely Deaths; with his Adventures in the Haunted Apartment, Discovery of the Fatal Closet, and appearance of the ghost of his Murdered Father; Relating, also how the Murderer was Brought to Justice, with his confession, and the Restoration of the Injured Orphan to his Title and Estates.

As it happens, this was nothing more than a pirated abridgement of Clara Reeve's *The Old English Baron*, and the hack writer did not even bother to change the names of the characters! A nineteenth century descendant of the shilling shocker was the 'penny dreadful' with its Gothic tales of terror for boys. These were often serials in weekly parts. Many of them were adventure stories such as *Jack Harkaway* or *Deadwood Dick*, but amongst the more horrific 'dreadfuls' were *Sweeney Todd*, *The Blue Dwarf*, and the immortal *Varney the Vampire; or, The Feast of Blood*.

Another by-product of the Gothic novel was its adaptation to the stage, and there were hundreds of Gothic melodramas. 'Monk' Lewis wrote many which must have severely taxed stage resources of scenery and machinery. His play *The Wood Daemon* or *The Clock has Struck* was a two–act 'Grand Romantic Melodrama', with 'a wonderful phantasmagoria of the supernatural, demons, witches, dragons, giants, set amid mountains and forest glooms and the great Gothic hall of a castle, illuminated by the blue lightning and heralded by the crashing thunder, with sacrifice of human victims to the Powers of Darkness . . .'

By the beginning of the nineteenth century, the Gothic impulse had influenced various literary forms. Already the sophistication of Augustan prose literature had given way to the romantic poetry of such authors as Byron, Coleridge and Shelley.

During that strange literary house party of highly-strung individuals (Byron, his physician John William Polidori, Shelley, Mary Godwin [Shelley's wife in all but name] and Mary's stepsister Claire Clairmont) at the Villa Diodati, Geneva, it was proposed that everyone should write a ghost story. The result was Mary Shelley's powerful book *Frankenstein* (first published 1818) and Polidori's *The Vampyre* (1819), both drawing upon folklore legend, to start a fashion for horror stories of monsters and vampires – still immensely popular themes in modern terror tales and movies.

Another recasting of the Gothic impulse was in the sensational atmospheric thrillers and crime stories of Edgar Allan Poe (1809 - 1849) in America. In *The Fall of the House of Usher*, *The Pit and the Pendulum*, and *Premature Burial*, all published in the 1840's, Poe adapted classic Gothic elements to the short story. In *The Murders in the Rue Morgue* and *The*

Purloined Letter, he adapted Gothic imagination to become the mystery element in crime detection.

In Britain, Wilkie Collins published *The Woman in White* in 1860 and *The Moonstone* in 1868, with plots as complex as any Gothic novel, but substituting for Gothic architecture a Gothic *atmosphere* of hidden mysteries, strange motives, crime, and sensational suspense. The modern detective thriller and romance clearly have roots in the Gothic novels of Poe and Wilkie Collins, and the convention of the old country mansion (instead of Gothic castle), culminating in such fine Gothic novels as Daphne du Maurier's *Rebecca* and a host of television serials like Susan Howatch's *Penmarric*. Modern popular romances involving an old country house or estate are known in the book trade as 'Gothics', and Mills and Boon have published many of them.

Let me now sketch briefly the Irish Gothic Connection.

In 1820, the impecunious Irish writer Charles Robert Maturin (1780 - 1824) achieved fame with publication of his powerful Gothic novel *Melmoth the Wanderer*. Maturin was born in Dublin and attended Trinity College at the age of 15, where he took his bachelor degree. He became a clergyman, curate at Loughren, and in 1804 at St. Peter's in Dublin. In addition to his clerical activities, he wrote poetry and novels. Lord Byron sponsored his play *Bertram*, and Edmund Kean played the lead in this melodrama about an Italian nobleman and his fair Imogene, in a setting of Gothic shipwreck, piracy, imprisonment, forced marriage and murder. In Maturin's novel *Melmoth the Wanderer*, there is also emphasis on episodes of Gothic terror, but this three volume Gothic achieved its major effect through a complex plot structure involving six interconnected stories.

Maturin had considerable literary talent and imaginative force, although *Melmoth the Wanderer* might be somewhat tedious to modern readers. He was admired by such writers of the time as Sir Walter Scott and the French novelist Balzac. Interestingly enough, Maturin's book must have been known to the later Irish writer Oscar Wilde (himself associated with Bram Stoker), who adopted the pseudonym 'Sebastian Melmoth' after his release from prison when he wrote *The Ballad of Reading Gaol*. Wilde himself had Gothic tendencies, and his book *The Picture of Dorian Gray* (1891) has the classic ingredients of the secret room at the top of the house, the supernatural portrait, and a melodramatic world of sophisticated elegance, strange sins, and creeping horror.

Somewhat between the gloomy atmosphere of Poe, Maturin and Wilkie Collins were the books of the Irish writer J. Sheridan Le Fanu (1814 - 1873). Born in Dublin, he too entered Trinity College, in 1833, and although trained as a lawyer commenced a career as a professional writer while still in college. The Gothic melancholy of his stories probably stemmed from the unhappy death of his wife in 1858. After that date, his works are permeated by a preoccupation with mystery, death and the supernatural. It is worth passing mention that his earlier story *The Purcell Papers* (1839) (first published in magazine form as *A Chapter in the History of the Tyrone Family)* must have provided Charlotte Brönte with the theme of her novel *Jane Eyre* - the young woman in love with an older man who keeps an insane wife hidden in his house - pure Gothic.

But Le Fanu's Gothic masterpiece is undoubtably his long 'short story' *Carmilla*, in which he revived the vampire theme developed from folklore by Polidori, Byron and others. *Carmilla* is a brilliantly atmospheric story of a female vampire, with a strong suggestion of Lesbian love. The plot is classic period Gothic, being set in a dreamlike landscape with an old castle in Styria, a beautiful vampire, and themes of love and death.

Carmilla was first published in 1871. It was read by another Dubliner – Bram Stoker, when he was a young part-time drama critic. It was to stay in his mind for twenty-five years before he wove the vampire theme into his own masterpiece *Dracula*.

Abraham (known as 'Bram') Stoker was born in Clontarf, Dublin, and entered Trinity College in November 1864, where he secured his M.A. Although originally a sickly child, he grew into an athletic giant and distinguished himself at Trinity in weightlifting and walking.

He also joined the Philosophical Society and became president. His first paper to the Society (perhaps prophetically) was titled 'Sensationalism in Fiction and Society'. He later spoke on various other subjects: King Lear, Shakespeare's fools, Keats, Shelley, and even Votes for Women. On his 25th birthday he also became Auditor of the Historical Society, a signal honour. A many sided man, Stoker championed the poetry of Walt Whitman (with whom he later became a firm friend), worked as a civil servant for ten tedious years at Dublin Castle, was unpaid drama critic for the *Dublin Evening Mail*, doing much to encourage appreciation of drama in general and the work of his idol Henry Irving in particular.

Five days after his marriage to Florence Balcombe the couple left for

England, where Bram took up an appointment as manager to Henry Irving, a post which he executed with distinction and loyalty until Irving's death in 1905.

In between strenuous theatrical duties, Stoker somehow found time to write short stories, mostly of a ghostly or thriller kind. In 1897, he published his major novel *Dracula*, which has had lasting influence on stories, plays and movies all over the world. The novel is pure Gothic - a tale of terror with a background of old Transylvania, Gothic castles, windswept English coast and graveyards, supernatural events, a pure heroine, horrendous villain, and chivalrous heroes.

The influences that culminated in this novel have been widely discussed. Stoker himself cited a nightmare after a late night supper of dressed crab, when he dreamed of a vampire king rising from the tomb. but we also know from his strange book of stories for children *Under the Sunset* (published in 1881) that themes of bloodletting and a terrifying Angel of Death were present years earlier, probably stimulated by his sickly childhood and his mother's frightening stories of a cholera plague in Sligo in 1832. Stoker had also read Le Fanu's vampire story *Carmilla*, and learned about a real life Dracula (Vlad Tepes or Vlad the Impaler) in fifteenth century Transylvania. Stoker's initial information on Transylvania surely came from the intrepid traveller Arminius Vambéry, whom he met at the Beefsteak Club in London in April 1890 after a performance of Irving in *The Dead Heart*, and again two years later at Trinity College, when Vambéry was awarded an honourary degree. Stoker even mentions 'my friend Arminius of Buda-Pesth University' in one chapter of *Dracula*. Another influence, an unconscious one, may have been the powerful personality of Henry Irving himself, who claimed all Stoker's energies and actions for so many years.

Although Stoker's work in the Theatre was his greatest achievement, his novel *Dracula* is undoubtedly a cornerstone in the history of the Gothic Novel, and this has been recognised in scores of articles, academic theses and critical works, many from the U.S.

Surprisingly enough this remarkable man has received little recognition in his own country. There is a flourishing W.B. Yeats and James Joyce industry, supported largely by American academics, but for a hundred years there has been no real interest in Ireland in a far more influential Irishman. Of course, Yeats and Joyce are giants of literature, whereas Stoker

DRACULA

6d.

BY

BRAM STOKER

6d.

WESTMINSTER

Archibald Constable & Co Ltd

2 WHITEHALL GARDENS

The cover of the first paperback edition of *Dracula*,
published in April 1901 at a price of 6 pence.

was not really in their class. Much of his other writing is marred by uneven style and much sentimentality, although always manifesting a great feeling for local colour, and a powerful, if sometimes feverish, imagination. *Dracula* is his major work, and in this book he created a mythology that has swept the world and probably had more influence than either Yeats or Joyce. Stoker's creation has a universal appeal at all levels, highbrow and lowbrow. The word 'Dracula' is known in nearly every country of the world and has generated hundreds of derivative plays, stories and movies, while at a scholarly level there are scores of academic studies and learned discussions of Stoker's motifs and motivations, invoking Freud and Jung and tortuous, often incomprehensible psychoanalytical interpretations.

Because of the lack of interest in Stoker in Ireland, it was left to a group of British enthusiasts to form a Dracula Society in England. I became a token Dublin member, but was unable to attract enough attention for a viable Dublin branch. However, in 1980, with a few fellow enthusiasts, I founded the Bram Stoker Society in Dublin to honour a great Irishman and explore Gothic themes in various media.

We have had many ups and downs. There was a pronounced drop in membership after the first year's reminder of subscription due, even though membership was a very moderate sum, less than the cost of a drink at the local public house, but we soon picked up again and organised many interesting lectures and film shows. For a time, we even achieved a strong connection with Stoker's old Philosophical Society at Trinity College, but after an initial enthusiastic welcome, problems of security and access to the 'Bram Stoker Room' housing my exhibition of Bram Stoker memorabilia resulted in withdrawing my collection and we went our separate ways.

However, the Trinity connection was later revived through the efforts of Secretary, Mr. David Lass, who formed a Bram Stoker Club at Trinity, providing a convenient locale for Bram Stoker Society meetings. The club has held regular meetings, lectures and film shows at Trinity.

In 1991, Mr. Dennis Mc Intyre, a founder member and Chairman of the Clontarf Historical Society, launched the Bram Stoker International Summer School, an annual event with lectures and exhibitions attracting participants from various countries, and promoting the associations of Clontarf with Bram Stoker, who was born there.

Also in 1991, I presented my Bram Stoker Collection (formerly at the Phil) to the newly founded Writers Museum in Parnell Square, Dublin, one of the most beautiful and elegant museums in Ireland. In June 1997, to mark the Dracula Centenary, the Museum mounted a special comprehensive Exhibition drawn from my Stoker Collection. The Exhibition was launched by Senator David Norris, a noted authority on James Joyce and also a relative of the Stoker family. In July, the Exhibition was augmented by a companion Exhibition of the haunted Gothic paintings of Jonathan Barry, a young Clontarf artist. The Irish Film Centre also arranged a special programme of films relating to Dracula and the Vampire superstition. This included a recently restored copy of the classic film *Nosferatu*, directed by F. W. Murnau, 1922.

All over the world Dracula themes continue to flourish in books, plays and movies. In 1992, yet another film version of Stoker's novel was released, directed by the famous film maker Francis Ford Coppola. On a more modest but no less valuable scale, the young Irish film maker Ian Graham, responsible for documentaries on Rex Ingram and James Joyce, collaborated with Radio Telefís Éireann to produce a compact but impressive film about Stoker titled *I Created Dracula*. Worthy of special mention too is the enthusiasm of Jonathan Barry, a young Clontarf born man, who made a home movie record of his own trip to Transylvania. In liberated Romania, there is now a regular tourist trade covering the locales of Jonathan Harker's route in Stoker's book and the castle of the real fifteenth century Dracula. Perhaps this centenary year of the publication of Dracula may inaugurate a comparable tourist trade to Ireland, for after all Stoker was a Dublin man.

What are we to make of this strange fascination which Stoker's book has exercised on popular literary taste and academic discussion for a century, outstripping all the other Gothic novels which have preceeded it? Without a lengthy analysis I would suggest briefly that the answer may lie in the decline of religious experience over two centuries of materialistic development. I believe that Gothic Literature represents a popular romantic restatement of the eternal theological mystery of the place of good and evil in human affairs, the fear of death and physical decay, and the religious problems of purgatory and damnation, with the hope of salvation. Its popular romantic form may be more effective than ponderous sermons which no longer strike terror to sinners.

This centenary of *Dracula*, also the 150th anniversary of Bram Stoker himself, the most influential author in the genre of the Gothic novel, could also signal a proper recognition of Stoker in his own country.

The Bram Stoker Society may be contacted through the Hon. Sec.,
David Lass,
Regent House,
Trinity College,
Dublin 2.

The Bram Stoker International Summer School can be contacted through the Director,
Dennis McIntyre,
101 Foxfield Grove,
Raheny,
Dublin 5.

7. BRAM STOKER AND THE TRADITION OF IRISH SUPERNATURAL FICTION

~ Albert Power ~

Bram Stoker's *Dracula* is the most famous Irish supernatural horror novel. It represents the high point in a tradition of ghostly fiction in Ireland which owes its origin to the English Gothic novel of the 1760s and 1790s.

The first Gothic novel, Horace Walpole's *The Castle of Otranto* (1764), set the trend for a host of successors and imitators, both good and bad. Walpole's tale is a farrago of murder and mystery set in a medieval fantasy world of ancient castles, ruined churches, dark forests, louring clouds that drape the moonlight, hidden chambers and unspeakable deeds of dastardliness. The typical cast of the Gothic novel, established by *The Castle of Otranto,* features vigorous villains, helpless heroines of surpassing beauty and unsullied virtue, and dashing heroes of limp imagination and questionable intelligence. Monastic corruption provides a plausible pillar for most of the plots. The most powerful of the Gothic novels are still read avidly today. These include Ann Radcliffe's *The Mysteries of Udolpho* (1764) and *The Italian* (1797) and Matthew Gregory Lewis's *The Monk* (1795). Perhaps the Gothic novel's most famous flowering is Mary Shelley's evocative and thought-stirring *Frankenstein* (1818).

Ireland's prime contribution came on the ebb tide of this great wave of the Gothic. Charles Robert Maturin (1780-1824) was a graduate of Trinity College Dublin and became a Church of Ireland clergyman, holding the curacy of St. Peter's, Dublin for many years up to his death. Maturin achieved little immediate or lasting success with his first Gothic novel *The Family of Montorio; or, The Fatal Revenge* (1807). However, with his fifth novel, *Melmoth the Wanderer* (1820), Maturin produced a masterpiece. This long and tortuous book, penned in a series of interlocking sub-narratives, describes the endless wanderings of a Faust-like villain, an Irishman named John Melmoth, who buys a hundred and fifty years of extra life from the devil, and spends most of that time trying to barter it. Curiously, the author's main interest seems to be in the histories of Melmoth's victims, rather than in the fate of the Wanderer himself. Working into the small hours, urged by indigence and inspired by brandy, Maturin's effusions often attain to a frenzied intensity. Despite a sometimes wearying prolixity, Maturin is master of the melancholy epigram.

"What a state of mind that must be, in which we are driven to wish we no longer had one! - when we would willingly forget that privilege of humanity, which only seems an undisputed title to superlative misery."

Melmoth's own story, set in Ireland, forms the outer framework of the novel. The sub-narratives are many and widely scattered in terms of setting. Of these, the most effective is a lengthy chunk called *The Spaniard's Narrative*. This describes the ingenious attempts made by young Alonzo de Monçada, the eldest, but illegitimate, son of a distinguished Spanish family, to extricate himself from a Spanish monastery to which his parents have consigned him, in an effort to hide his birth. Set in eighteenth century Madrid, it is a protracted story of deception and cruelty rich in vivid scenes of horror. Yet one is driven to wonder whether Maturin's inspiration may not have stemmed from closer to home. Support for this view is lent by Maturin's frequent bolstering of his lurid vignettes by footnoted allusions to similar scenes in Ireland, which either he himself had witnessed or else had had recounted to him. One such footnote relates the revolting butchery with pikes of Lord Arthur Kilwarden, Lord Chief Justice of Ireland, during Robert Emmet's abortive insurrection of 1803, a sight so shocking that it permanently blasted the mind of a neighbouring artisan, who, unhappily, chanced to look out of his window at just the wrong moment.

The death scene of a descendant of Melmoth, in a dirty hovel on the coast of County Wicklow, features a grim parody of a certain Irish type - the Gombeen Man, also a leading character in Bram Stoker's earliest novel *The Snake's Pass* (1891).

Charles Robert Maturin died in 1824, having enjoyed little celebrity during his own lifetime. The poet, James Clarence Mangan (1803-1848), who had known him, wrote:-

"He - in his own dark way - understood many people; but nobody understood him in any way. And therefore it was that he, this man of the highest genius, Charles Robert Maturin, lived unappreciated - and died unsympathised with, uncared for, uninquired after - and not only forgotten because he had never been thought about."

Neither should we forget James Clarence Mangan himself, blood brother to the doom-depressed progenitors of the Irish ghost story. Best known now, if at all, for his poems, particularly *Dark Rosaleen*, Mangan lived a dark, tormented life, racked by alcohol and opium and frustrated love. His several strange tales and exotic poems attest to an inner fire which drove and at last consumed him. In his later years, prematurely aged, he could be seen stalking around Trinity College Dublin, with his thin gaunt face, his wild grey hair thrown back, clad in a long white single-seam garment like a winding sheet. John Mitchel, the Young Irelander, who knew him at this time, epitomised the very essence of the man in one succinct image : "In his arms he held a great book, and all his soul was in that book."

Maturin's *Melmoth The Wanderer* represents the last great blossoming of the Gothic novel. Throughout the 1830s and 1840s the miniaturised horror tapestries of Edgar Allan Poe (1809-1849) were pointing in a new direction. Though preserving the dark embroideries of Gothic horror, Poe introduced a new personalised intensity and gave voice to his grim imaginings through the vehicle of the short story. It was through the short story also that the most famous Irish writer of ghostly fiction vented in literature his nightmare genius. This was Joseph Sheridan Le Fanu (1814-1873), a barrister turned journalist, like Maturin a Dublin-man and a graduate of Trinity College.

Le Fanu was born in Dublin, spent his youth in County Limerick, then returned to Dublin where he lived in Merrion Square, after the premature death of his young wife in 1858 becoming a virtual recluse. His twin areas of speciality were the mystery novel, in which form he ran Wilkie Collins close, and the supernatural short story where he is unparalleled. In his earlier years Le Fanu sought to specialise in the romantic historical novel, transferring to his own country the already proven techniques of Sir Walter Scott : hence his first two novels, *The Cock and Anchor* (1845), set in early eighteenth century Dublin, and *The Fortunes of Colonel Torlough O'Brien* (1847), a tale about the Jacobite Wars. In his early short stories, first published in the Dublin University Magazine, then posthumously in book form as *The Purcell Papers* (1880) - after the stories' linking narrative character, Fr. Francis Purcell - Le Fanu tackles, in allegorical fashion, the theme of the demise of the Great House and of the old Irish Catholic aristocracy. Though the writing style in these early tales lacks the terseness and refinement of Le Fanu's later work, the supernatural element in such stories as *The Drunkard's Dream* and *Schalken the Painter* is particularly chilling.

Le Fanu drew extensively on his childhood experience in County Limerick for some of his later folklore-based ghost stories. Stories such as *The White Cat of Drumgunniol, The Child that Went with the Fairies, Sir Dominic's Bargain, Ultor de Lacey* and *Stories of Lough Guir* cleverly rework the legends and superstitions of the mid-West.

However, Le Fanu's best writings are unrelated to the folk tradition. Unlike Edgar Allan Poe, they avoid the usual trappings and style of the Gothic, and so, in large degree, outlive the era in which they were written. Like James Clarence Mangan, Le Fanu's most memorable outpourings are tormented : his conscience-spawned spectres show us for the first time the ghost of the *mind*, which is yet, disquietingly, sometimes seen by others too, so that at the end we know not for certain whether the tormenting spirit comes from within or without.

In 1872, the year before his death, Le Fanu brought out a collection of short stories called *In A Glass Darkly*. These included *The Familiar, Mr. Justice Harbottle* and *Green Tea* (ghost stories), *The Room in the Dragon Volant* (a long murder-mystery story), and *Carmilla* (a vampire tale set in modern Slovenia). These stories are among Le Fanu's greatest, and indeed, rank, by any reckoning, among the foremost in the ghost story genre. *Carmilla* is of special significance as being the first treatment of the vampire legend by an Irish writer, and, arguably, was a crucial influence on Bram Stoker's *Dracula*.

Bram Stoker (1847-1912) embodies what might be termed the third generation in the tradition of Irish supernatural fiction. His background, middle-class Protestant, and graduate of Trinity College Dublin, closely resembles those of Maturin and Le Fanu. In 1879, after a lightning romance and hurried marriage to Florence Balcombe, formerly the girlfriend of Oscar Wilde, Bram Stoker threw over his humdrum job as a civil servant in Dublin Castle, to take on the strenuous role of manager of actor Henry Irving's Lyceum Theatre Company in London.

It was a demanding job which involved long hours and often little thanks, leaving Stoker with scant time to pursue his writing. Indeed, it was not until Irving's death in 1905 that Stoker became a full-time writer when the demise of the Lyceum Theatre Company left him with no other means of subsistence. Stoker himself died in 1912, so he had very little real opportunity to develop his skills as a writer. On this account, one often finds an unevenness in Stoker's work. At times it is taut and vivid, at others tedious and turgid. Given the constraints under which Stoker laboured for most of his life, it is little short of a marvel that he found time to write anything at all!

Stoker's writings can be divided, broadly, into three categories : romance novels, horror novels and short stories with supernatural elements, and general writings. His romance novels are ably written with strong sentimentalised plots. They include *The Watter's Mou'* (1894), *The Shoulder of Shasta* (1895), *Miss Betty* (1898), *The Man* (1905) and *Lady Athlyne* (1908). In part a romance novel, in part adventure story, and in part a disguised autobiography, is *The Mystery of the Sea* (1902), a lengthy novel set against the backdrop of Cruden Bay on the east coast of Scotland which Stoker had first discovered in 1890 and thereafter visited often, alternatively as a holiday resort and a scenic workshop. It was in Cruden Bay, modern research has now shown, that most of his famous novel *Dracula* was written.

His general works include a two-volume *Personal Reminiscences of Sir Henry Irving* (1906), a lecture pamphlet *A Glimpse of America* (1886) and a collation of renowned historical frauds called *Famous Impostors* (1910). Unique among his general writings is Stoker's first published book, and one which best expresses his Irish roots, for it is, in fact, a reference book for Irish civil servants and law clerks : *The Duties of Clerks of Petty Sessions in Ireland* (1879). With its generous festoonings of dull details, amply supported by quotations from statute and regulation, about dog licences, cattle trespasses, summonses and stamp duties, it could not be further removed from the Gothic world of *Dracula*. Stoker began writing this book after he had been appointed Inspector of Petty Sessions in 1876, essentially to ease the load of the unfortunate clerks who at that time had no reference works other than a mound of precedents and ancient statutes. By the time the book was eventually published by John Falconer of 53 Upper Sackville Street in 1879, Stoker was miles away in a new life with Irving at the Lyceum Theatre in London. In later years he was to look on this fledgling book as "dry as dust", and came to disregard it as a legitimate work altogether. Seemingly, though, the clerks of petty sessions found it helpful, and there is some evidence that when the British administration moved out of Dublin Castle, and, indeed, left Ireland, in 1922, copies of this seminal text found their way over to the Four Courts, where at least a few of them survived the bombing of the Civil War.

Though he had already published at least four short stories in his twenties, *The Crystal Cup* (1872), *The Primrose Path*, *Buried Treasure* and *The Chain of Destiny* (all 1875), Stoker's first book collection was a set of macabre supernatural fairy tales, *Under the Sunset* (1882). These tales, anticipating in darker hue the type of fables for which Oscar Wilde was later to become celebrated, are set in a remote never-never world called The Land Under The Sunset. There is a lyrical, poetic touch to these stories, far removed from Stoker's heavily textured style in *Dracula* and the horror novels. In essence, they are moral fables, probably intended for children, but rather grimmer than would appeal to the tastes of any normal child. One need but instance the story *The Castle of the King*, in which a grief-tormented poet journeys through the Valley of the Shadow of Death to try and retrieve his deceased loved one, only to be stricken down himself; or the story *The Invisible Giant*, in which a deadly plague in the form of a sightless, unseen giant overwhelms an entire city for its wickedness, to get some idea of the book's general flavour.

It has been suggested that in writing this collection, and in particular *The Invisible Giant*, Stoker was influenced by an account earlier written by his mother, Charlotte Stoker, of a cholera epidemic in Sligo in 1832, which she had herself lived through as a child. Mrs. Stoker's report of how the cholera devastated half the town, and, especially, of the growing inhumanity in privation of former neighbours to each other, makes harrowing reading. Such descriptions as the following would not be amiss from the pen of Maturin :

> "One action I vividly remember. A poor traveller was taken ill on the roadside some miles from the town, and how did those samaritans tend him? They dug a pit and with long poles pushed him living into it, and covered him up quick, alive. Severely, like Sodom, did our city pay for such crimes."

Stoker's next foray into the macabre came in 1891 with *The Snake's Pass*, a novel set in the West of Ireland. This combines a routine love interest with the sinister legend of the King of the Snakes and a treasure lost by the French army in 1798. The Snake's Pass, called the Shleenanaher - a literal translation of the Irish *slí na n'athar* - is part of a mountain said to be the scene of a confrontation between St. Patrick and the King of the Snakes. The mountain is called Knockcalltecrore, an anglicisation of the Irish words '*cnoc na caillte coróin óir*', which mean, literally, 'the hill of the lost crown of gold'. The principal geological feature of this mountain is a treacherous shifting bog, which Stoker implies is the latter-day form assumed by the still active King of the Snakes. In his depiction of Black Murtagh, ('the Gombeen Man'), a greedy and unscrupulous moneylender, Stoker writes with particular vividness and intensity. In a sense, Black Murtagh is the archetype of evil and so prefigures, in character if not in power, the awesome Count Dracula himself.

Dracula was completed in 1897, though we now know this most famous of Stoker's novels took several years to research and write. Then came *The Jewel of Seven Stars,* in 1903, a novel with a reincarnation theme, in which wicked Queen Tera's complex plans for a second coming wreak havoc on the lives of the explorers who discover her hidden tomb in Egypt's Valley of the Sorcerer and take her mummified body back to London. *Snowbound*, a collection of short stories from a fictitious theatrical company, followed in 1908, and *The Lady of the Shroud* in 1909. This novel has a theme and setting not unlike *Dracula*. A beautiful young princess in the make-believe Balkan kingdom of the Land of the Blue Mountains assumes the role of a she-vampire for political reasons. A young Scot, who inherits a castle there, falls in love with her and helps to deliver her people from the marauding Turks. This novel is distinguished by some highly improbable melodrama. An example is a frantic scene in which a character called the Gospodar jumps from a cliff, breaking his fall by clutching the branches of trees growing out perpendicularly from the cliff face, and lands safely on the ground after severing a Turkish invader's head with his scimitar while in mid-flight. Another scene, lending a quaintly - for the time - contemporary touch, involves a daring rescue operation by aeroplane, in which the aircraft contrives to land very adroitly on top of a

prison wall!

Last came *The Lair of the White Worm* (1911), an extraordinary story about a huge white worm which has survived for thousands of years in a labyrinth of caverns in the south of England and transforms itself into a beautiful young woman, Lady Arabella March, who sports slinky white dresses and has an abiding dread of mongooses - the bane of snakes. This novel, written in a jerky, irregular style (not enhanced by further pruning by subsequent paperback publishers), since Stoker was terminally ill at the time of its composition, contains a wide gamut of highly unusual characters, including Oolanga, a baleful Negro, and Edgar Caswell, a local madman who owns a castle and flies a huge kite from its battlements - to scare away the birds.

At the time of his death, in April 1912, Stoker (according to his widow, Florence) had been planning the publication of three volumes of short stories earlier published by him piecemeal in various periodicals and magazines. One volume appeared posthumously, with an introduction by Florence Stoker, under the title *Dracula's Guest and Other Weird Stories*. The opening story, *Dracula's Guest*, had originally been intended as an introductory sequence for the novel *Dracula*, but was excised at the behest of the publisher due to the novel's already considerable length. It is difficult to guess what might have formed the contents of Stoker's other two anthologies, since Stoker's writings in shorter form were multifarious and published in numerous different periodicals.

Likewise difficult to assess is the exact significance of his being Irish on Bram Stoker's writings. One can see it clearly enough in *Under the Sunset* and *The Snake's Pass*, but otherwise specifically Irish incursions are not easy to discern. True, there are Gaelic characterisations in *The Mystery of the Sea* and *The Watter's Mou'*, and a large element of stage Irishness in *The Man from Shorrox's*, a semi-whimsical, semi-grisly short story published in 1894. The charge of stage Irishness or blarney can be levelled at certain of Stoker's writings. Unlike Maturin and Le Fanu, Stoker spent most of his life in England, mingling in society circles, and so was out of touch with direct inspiration from his native country.

At one time it was fashionable to conjecture that during Le Fanu's later years and while Stoker was a young man living in Dublin the two must have met. Attractive though this speculation is, I am not aware that there is any evidence to support it. That Le Fanu's writings may have influenced Stoker's is more likely. Certainly, there is a close resemblance between Le Fanu's short story *An Account of Some Strange Disturbances in Aungier Street* (1853) and Stoker's *The Judge's House* (1891). Both stories concern the supernatural prowlings of a wicked 'hanging judge'; in each case the house possesses a lurid portrait of the judge which exerts a disturbing influence on the house's occupants; and in each case also the judge becomes embodied in the form of a grotesque and menacing rat. Also, Le Fanu's *Carmilla* which appeared in 1872, detailing the wiles of a female vampire in modern Slovenia, stirs parallel echoes in parts of *Dracula's Guest*, and was demonstrably an inspiration for the novel *Dracula* itself.

But more compellingly than any of these academic-type comparisons, Bram Stoker's Irishness manifested in his staunch and generous personality which spilled over into his characterisations in fiction. Bram Stoker was an archetype of uprightness, steadfastness and decency. He was ever a man of honour, a loyal friend, a tireless worker and unflagging supporter of those whose causes he espoused. Stories abound of Stoker's heroism and selflessness : how, for example, in 1882, he dived into the Thames from a steamer to try and save a man from drowning, but failed in the attempt; of his kindly advices to actresses Genevieve Ward and Ellen Terry when time could ill be spared for the giving of advice; of his tireless labours as Theatre Manager for actor Henry Irving, a man difficult to work for by all accounts, whom he served unstintingly for twenty-seven years.

Despite the erotic attributions of vampire blood guzzling, which Stoker does not strive to conceal, the man himself was very much a moralist, a supporter of censorship, and a devoted idealiser of women - though the then conventional image of woman as a domestic, supportive entity to be protected would have appealed to his sense of the proper.

In his obituary notice in *The Times* it was justly said of Bram Stoker : "Few men have played the part of Fidus Achates to a great personality with more gusto." Nor was it without reason that Walt Whitman, the American poet whose works Stoker so stoutly championed in his student days, referred to him as "a broth of a boy".

These personality traits inevitably seep into his writing. The romance novels drip with them. And even in the horror novels we invariably find a select group of staunch, high-principled men limbering themselves up to take on such diverse embodiments of evil as Black Murtagh, Dracula, and the White Worm. In his choice of plot Stoker is more akin to the Gothic writers than to Le Fanu. Unlike Le Fanu, he does not engulf us in half-hidden questions of metaphysics, nor trouble us with the torments of a supernaturally pestered conscience. The conflicts of which he treats are primal - good against evil, right against wrong. But for all that, he wrenches the reader into the thick of the struggle, forcing a keen emotional involvement with the outcome of the fray. The comment made by Harry Ludlam, author of the first biography of Bram Stoker in 1962, about his collection *Under the Sunset* :

> " . . . it was written with a love of words and the sympathy and understanding of the
> big heart"

- is equally applicable to all Stoker's fiction.

There have been other stalwarts also in the tradition of Irish supernatural fiction. Foremost among these is Mrs. J.H. Riddell (born Charlotte Cowan, in Carrickfergus, Co. Antrim, 1832-1906), who, against adverse personal circumstances, became a distinguished doyenne of Victorian letters, specialising in probing novels about commercial life and some excellent ghost stories. *The Last Squire of Ennismore*, *Hertford O'Donnell's Warning* and *Old Mrs. Jones* are among her legacy to ghostly literature. Then there was the doom-propelled Co. Limerick-man, Fitzjames O'Brien (1828-1862), whose sensitively wrought and craftily turned fantasy tales, such as *The Diamond Lens* and *The Wondersmith*, evoke the enchanted nightmare worlds of Ambrose Bierce and Guy de Maupassant. His own life was shattered prematurely on the battlefields of the American Civil War.

Nor can we forget the versatile Lord Dunsany (1878-1957). Lord Dunsany did not write many ghost stories in the conventional vein, but many indeed are the fables flung from his pen about the activities of mythical gods and the fantastic effusions of boozy reminiscence associated with a man called Jorkens, of - or *not quite* of - the Billiards Club! Names like Skarl, Mung, Mana-Yood-Sushai, Leothric and Nuth ring shimmeringly like silver bells in his rich and singing prose. Then there was the Co. Louth-born author, Dorothy Macardle (1889-1958), whose earlier years were taken up with the struggle for Irish Independence and whose first ghost stories were written in Mountjoy Gaol. In her later years she wrote an enduring account of those troubled years of conflict in *The Irish Republic* (1951), and also penned some excellent novels of the supernatural and macabre, such as *Dark Enchantment* (1953) and *Uneasy Freehold* or *The Uninvited* (1942). This latter book was memorably translated to cinema in 1944, by Paramount in a film called *"The Uninvited"*, directed by Lewis

Allen and featuring Ray Milland.

The fantasy writings of Mervyn Wall (1908-1997) fall more into the class of satirical comedy. His celebrated novels *The Unfortunate Fursey* (1946) and *The Return of Fursey* (1948) amuse rather than frighten us in their portrayal of a foolish middle-aged monk in twelfth century Ireland, his strange adventures and the supernatural tribulations by which he is beset. Yet no reader can overlook the author's pointedly sarcastic allusions to the oppressive cultural climate in which these novels were written. On the other hand, Mervyn Wall's own long association with the civil service, for which he worked for many years, begets an acute understanding of the drudgery, dispiritedness and sheer tedium which infests that mundane world. In what I might term his serious novels, treating of this environment, *Leaves for the Burning* (1952), *No Trophies Raise* (1956) and *Hermitage* (1978), we are drawn into a grim and Gothic atmosphere which, though free from the supernatural, recalls at once all the torment of Maturin and Le Fanu. In a strange way, it is the humdrum world of Stoker's *The Duties of Clerks of Petty Sessions in Ireland* which Mervyn Wall embroiders with the troubled trappings of nightmare; the more exotic realms of Castle Dracula and the Land of the Blue Mountains are not for him. The passing of Mervyn Wall on 19th May 1997 deprived Irish literature of one of its most distinctive, if sparingly spoken, voices.

The writers so fleetingly discussed in this essay have an affinity with their material and an earnestness of expression not always to found in the ghostly tale. It is as if the supernatural had a secret appeal to the dark and mysterious workings of a certain type of Irish mind. Styles may vary, but the message meant to be imparted is ever a sincere one. In a generous tribute to Le Fanu, whose style and techniques markedly influenced his own writing, the English ghost story writer M.R. James (1862-1936) observed :

"As to his [Le Fanu's] peculiar power : I think the origin of it is not far to seek. Le Fanu had both French and Irish blood in his veins, and in his works I seem to see both strains coming out, though the Irish predominates. The indefinable melancholy which the air of Ireland and its colouring inspire - a melancholy which inspires many Irish writers - is caught by Le Fanu and fixed in words with an almost complete success. He dwells very fondly and very frequently on sunset scenes over a horizon of dark hanging woods, on moonlight shining on a winding river with wooded banks, on a heavily-timbered park, a black tarn in a lonely glen, an old air heard in the distance at night, a ruined chapel or manor-house, a torchlight funeral

in a gloomy church."

These are attributions also to be found in the writings of Maturin and Stoker.

We are far more familiar today with the Celtic twilight world of W.B. Yeats, Lady Gregory, J.M. Synge and Douglas Hyde. But the writers whose lives and works I have so lightly sketched are kinspeople of the same tradition, representing its unique verdure in darker, more sinister forms, deep rooted in the raw, rich soil of the Irish soul. Let us hope that, through the nurture of appreciation, this strange blossom will continue to flourish, and so enchant us still in the times to come.

8. THE BEETLE AND DRACULA

~ Richard Dalby ~

The success of Bram Stoker's *Dracula* in the summer of 1897 inspired an immediate spate of weird fantasy and horror novels. Some of these, like Florence Marryat's *The Blood of the Vampire*, soon disappeared from view, but one title quickly stood out from the rest and became a runaway best-seller : this was *The Beetle* by Richard Marsh.

According to literary folklore, Marsh's novel was written following a wager with Stoker, each man agreeing to produce a supernatural novel by a certain time. It is known that they were acquaintances rather than close friends (there is only one short letter to Stoker from Marsh in the Brotherton Collection, requesting four seats at the Lyceum), but this anecdote is certainly apocryphal. Whereas Stoker took several years to research and write *Dracula*, there is little doubt that Marsh wrote *The Beetle* at his usual speed following the publication of the vampire masterpiece.

There has been nothing quite like *The Beetle*, before or since. The beetle of the title is a malignant, deformed creature inhabited by the soul of an Ancient Egyptian princess, a metamorphosis of an avatar of Isis, which can turn at will into a scarab-like insect, or alternatively into man or woman, or an enigmatic amalgam of both: sometimes ageless and sexless, sometimes pulsating with libido, and with strong hypnotic powers. As with *Dracula*, the story is told by the multi-narrational method, and the first part is the best, where a tramp breaks into a seemingly empty suburban villa only to discover he is not alone! The main plot centres round a Member of Parliament who in his youth was held prisoner, drugged, in Cairo and forced to watch nameless orgies with young English girl tourists as sacrificial victims. A chase by train from St. Pancras forms part of the novel's exciting climax.

Obviously, with all these scintillating ingredients, the book's success with the Victorian public was assured. "*The Beetle* is as horrid as one could wish", claimed the *Daily Chronicle*; and the *Glasgow Herald* enthused:

"The weird horror of this Being grows upon the reader. It is difficult, if not impossible, to lay down this book once begun. Mr. Bram Stoker's effort of the imagination was not easy to beat, but Mr. Marsh, so to speak, has out-Heroded Herod."

The first impression, published by Skeffington in September 1897, sold out immediately. Today it is as scarce as its running mate, *Dracula*, and is a much more attractively bound volume, in its blood-red cloth with a large beetle scampering across the front cover. There are four illustrations by John Williamson, and one of these (the frontispiece) was reproduced on the front cover of some of the later editions. Second, third and fourth impressions followed quickly in October, November, and December 1897. Both *Dracula* and *The Beetle* remained two of the top favourite 'horror' best-sellers throughout the Edwardian era, with Marsh's opus leading the field. By 1913, The Beetle had reached its 15th printing, whereas *Dracula* was only into its 10th. T.Fisher Unwin had now taken over *The Beetle* from Skeffington, and incorporated it into the attractive Adelphi Library (with gilt decorated cloth, vastly preferable to the indifferent Constable and Rider bindings) alongside George Moore and George MacDonald. Among other editions which I have collected in the past twenty years is the pocket sized George Newnes reprint (Sevenpenny Series in red cloth gilt) which has a superb colourful pictorial dust jacket by Stanley L. Wood.

The Beetle also preceded *Dracula* in the cinema. Its only appearance on film was in a long-lost 1919 silent movie, directed by Alexander Butler, and starring Heyden Foster as the M.P. and Leal Douglas in the title role. Why the story has never been remade as a 'talkie' is an inexplicable mystery. Abraham Sofaer and Catherine Lacey starred in a stage version at the Strand Theatre, London, in 1928.*

The novel has been consistently reprinted ever since. Later editions appeared in Grayson's Library in the late-20s and 30s, and went into paperback in the late-50s and mid-60s. The brothers Sir Hugh and Graham Greene always felt that *The Beetle* was a book which should never be out of print, and included it in their omnibus of four classic novels *Victorian Villainies* (Viking/Penguin - now available in many remainder bookshops, an excellent bargain at under £5) A reviewer of this omnibus (in *The Times*) described *The Beetle* as "one of the few stories that genuinely tingled my spine without indulging in over-the-top ugliness."

* The story appears to have inspired a 1968 film titled *The Blood Beast* (directed by Vernon Sewell) in which there is a metamorphosis of a human being into a giant moth.

Original artwork for *The Beetle* by Claudia Andrei

The mysterious Richard Marsh was always secretive about his early life. In scattered works of reference, his true name and date of birth are not given; and virtually nothing is revealed in his *Who's Who* entry apart from an abbreviated list of books (less than half his total) and intriguing recreations:

> "He loved them all — cricket, billiards, chess, bridge, motoring and a dozen more. A clumsy but enthusiastic student of whatever made for proficiency in the fine art of doing nothing."

Curiously, he has no entries in the *Encyclopaedia of Mystery and Detection*, *Twentieth Century Crime and Mystery Writers*, *The Longman Companion to Victorian Fiction* (1988), and *The 1890s* (1993), although he certainly deserves a place in all these hefty volumes, and many more.

The best description of Richard Marsh can be found in *The Attempted Rescue* (1966), the autobiography of Robert Aickman, his grandson and enthusiastic collector of Marsh's first editions, and one of Britain's most gifted modern writers of 'strange stories'. Here he is briefly portrayed as a large, plump man, with a moustache and a monocle. Other details are sketchy, and Aickman did not know the first names of his grandfather's parents, though his real surname was revealed as 'Heldmann'.

Following the clues given by Aickman, I tracked down Marsh's birth certificate in St. Catherine's House (London) over ten years ago. This reveals that he was born Richard Bernard Heldmann on 12 October 1857, at 23 Adelaide Road, St. John's Wood in London. His parents were Joseph Heldmann, a lace merchant, and Emma Heldmann "formerly Marsh".

Robert Aickman and Sir Hugh Greene both alleged that Marsh was educated at Eton and Oxford, but this is completely unsubstantiated. There is no record that any member of the Heldmann family attended either in the late 19th century.

Following a few short stories written for boys' magazines in his teens, his professional literary career started - under his own name, 'Bernard Heldmann' - at the age of twenty-three early in 1881. *Dorrincourt, Boxhall School, Expelled*, and *The Belton Scholarship* (dedicated to his cousin "Miss Marsh of Nottingham") are all entertaining school stories for boys; while *The Mutiny on Board the Ship Leander* is a gripping sea yarn dedicated to George A. Henty.

Following the publication of his next book, *Daintree*, in 1883, he disappeared completely for nearly ten years. No fresh Heldmann titles were published, though the original six remained very popular and went into several new and cheaper editions. For such a busy and prolific author, it is very unlikely that he would have ceased writing altogether. Probably he used an unknown pseudonym (impossible to detect now) during this missing decade. Although he never changed his name by deed-poll, the 'Heldmann' persona was not used again, and is not mentioned in any reference book with an entry on Marsh.

The name 'Richard Marsh' (taken from his mother's side of the family) appeared quietly and gradually with a series of tales in several popular magazines in 1891 and 1892, notably *The Strand* with *A Vision of the Night* (Christmas Number, 1892). Several anonymous supernatural stories like *A Set of Chessmen* in the *Cornhill* were revealed to be by Marsh only when they later appeared in his collections at the turn of the century.

The first two Marsh novels, *The Devil's Diamond* and *The Mahatma's Pupil*, were both published by Henry and Co. in 1893. Then his great success came with *The Beetle*, the seventh Marsh novel. Aickman recalled that Marsh sold *The Beetle* outright (as Fergus Hume had done with *The Mystery of a Hansom Cab*) "in order to keep his family for a week or two". By this time Marsh was married with four or five children to support.

He tried to duplicate the success of *The Beetle* with another occult thriller *Tom Ossington's Ghost*, published in June 1898. This concerns two young women who take up residence in the house formerly occupied by an eccentric miser, Ossington; after suffering nocturnal alarms and supernatural visitations, they finally unearth his hidden treasure. It was quite popular, and reprinted several times, but never achieved the high sales of *The Beetle*. Other novels in a similar vein include *The Joss: A Reversion* (1902), *The Death-Whistle* (1903), and *A Spoiler of Men* (1905) where a mad scientist transforms those obstructing him into quivering simulacra of men.

Another rare title is *Curios*, published by John Long in November 1898. *The Spectator* was enthusiastic :

> "Mr. Richard Marsh, an admitted expert in the art of scalp-tightening, gives fresh proofs of his skill in *Curios*, the strange adventures - grim, grotesque and gruesome - of two bachelors. The adventures are especially good."

One of his most touching and thought-provoking fantasies was *A*

Second Coming (Grant Richards, 1900), with Christ suddenly returning to earth, this time in London. The novel is told as a succession of vignettes and incidents involving people of various social levels. He is finally rejected by the disbelieving majority, including an Anglican archbishop and a cardinal. (No doubt the year 2000 will see a resurgence in new Second Coming stories.)

Besides his large output of novels (over sixty in little more than twenty years), Richard Marsh wrote hundreds of short stories for all the popular monthly magazines: *Pearsons, Pall Mall, Harmsworths, Storyteller, Royal, Windsor, Grand,* and no less than sixty for *The Strand* alone.

Among his many short ghost and horror stories which were reprinted from magazines in such collections as *Marvels and Mysteries*, *The Seen and the Unseen*, and *Both Sides of the Veil*, are *The Fifteenth Man* (a rugby match is won for his side by the ghost of a recently deceased player), *The Adventure of Lady Wishaw's Hand* (a perfectly preserved hand dating from the 14th century still has the power to strangle people), *A Psychological Experiment* (fiendish retribution involving snakes and lizards, and a monstrous jack-in-the-box), *The Haunted Chair* (a ghost story in *Harmsworths London Magazine*, January 1902), and *A Silent Witness* (catalepsy and the threat of premature burial).

Although Richard Marsh is chiefly remembered today for his bizarre horror stories, he also made a strong mark in the crime and detective genre, with titles like *Chase of the Ruby* and *An Aristocratic Detective*. Two of his most memorable characters were the accomplished teacher and lip-reader Judith Lee, a very unusual detective whose first twelve adventures ran in *The Strand* magazine from August 1911 to August 1912; and the ingenious junior clerk who appeared as Sam Briggs, His Book (1912), followed by another long series in *The Strand* (January to December 1915), published by Unwin as *Sam Briggs V.C.*

For over two decades Marsh wrote at furious speed and tremendous pressure, always in a tiny handwriting reminiscent of that of Charlotte Bronte. At least half of his novels were popular romances with titles like *The Magnetic Girl* and *Love in Fetters*.

He travelled abroad for at least three months each year, and spent every penny he earned without much difficulty. The family lived at Three Bridges, Sussex, for some years, then moved to a larger house, The Ridge at Haywards Heath. It was here that Richard Marsh died suddenly from heart failure, on 9 August 1915. So great was his industry that no fewer than eleven new books were published after his death.

Thanks to *The Beetle*, the name of Richard Marsh will never be completely forgotten. Most of his other works are well worth searching out, though the crime, mystery and horror titles are now all very elusive. After helping Robert Aickman build up his unequalled (and probably unique) set of Marsh first editions, I concentrated on collecting most of the fantasy and horror titles for myself. There are more than enough short supernatural stories to make a fine collection which is scheduled for publication by the Ghost Story Press in 1997, the centenary of both *Dracula* and *The Beetle*.

* * * * * *

Adapted from his article "Richard Marsh and *The Beetle*", which included a facsimile of a letter from Richard Marsh to Bram Stoker dated 9 June 1902. (*Antiquarian Book Monthly Review*, April 1986)

9. THE ENIGMA OF THE COUNT OF ST. GERMAIN

~ Vincent Hillyer ~

Almost all literary, television and movie vampires are modelled after one historical figure - the infamous Vlad the Impaler, Prince Dracula of Wallachia, who made life tough for the Turks during his brief lifetime. As we are all aware, he was born in Sighisoara, Transylvania in 1431 and presumably perished in 1476. When he abandoned his Orthodox faith to marry the sister of King Matthias of Hungary, the church cursed him to wander the earth forever as a vampire. The Ottoman Turks truly believed Dracula was one of the Undead – possessed of supernatural powers that rendered him impossible to defeat in battle, and they held him in great dread. Dracula basked in his profane reputation, and did all he could to encourage it.

But - to the chagrin of many of us, he wasn't really a vampire.

There was, though, an historical figure who might have been. One who was endowed with all the classic attributes of the traditional vampire. But oddly history does not label him as such. He was called many things during his celebrated eighteenth century appearances. Some contemporaries dubbed him a charlatan. But many others swore he was a truly immortal magus. Even his detractors were forced to acknowledge him as a most remarkable man, literally one of a kind. He shunned the sunlight, was never observed eating or drinking, wore black, and was reported to be over 2,000 years old. Everyone said he was immortal. But . . . they never said he was a vampire.

Until now.

Perhaps the strangest man who ever lived, a true enigma to historians, was . . . or is . . . the Count of St. Germain. An alchemist - magician who became the darling of every royal court in Europe in the years preceding the French Revolution, his arcane reputation was so great and widespread it has spilled over into our times. Today, as then, he is revered by many as some kind of supernal being. Theosophists regard him as one of the great "Secret Masters". A Los Angeles cult with roots going back to the 1930's believes St. Germain is a God-sent prophet capable of granting dispensations to those who pray in his name.

Who is the man who could so easily enchant royalty and later chroniclers of the ensuing centuries? Did he really perform all the incredible feats attributed to him? Many have said a most emphatic yes! But his occult successes and amazing exploits are not hearsay handed down from one generation to another. They are all well documented, and supported by historical evidence. There is no mystery that he did the things he was reported to do.

The *mystery* lies in discovering who this man is. Like all else about St. Germain, the dates of his birth and death remain a riddle. There are many claims. Some historians insist that he was born around 1710 in to the noble Rakoczi family of Transylvania. The Rakoczi's ruled that kingdom until they were deposed by Austria before St. Germain's birth.

Other sources say that St. Germain was the illegitimate son of the promiscuous Queen of Spain. The popular American author, Chelsea Quinn Yarbro, who has made St. Germain the hero/vampire of her many colourful and absorbing historical/romance/horror novels, theorises that he was the well educated son of wealthy Czech jewel merchants, who delighted in mystifying his generation. In any case, it is known that he frequently called himself Count Rakoczi, one of the many aliases he used during his eighteenth century prominence. He encouraged the rumour that he was two thousand years old, often implying that he had been a guest along with Christ at the wedding feast in Cana. Always ambiguous about his past, St. Germain never publicly denied the widely circulated gossip that he had once been an intimate friend of King Solomon and the Queen of Sheba.

Reinforcing his claim to endless life, St. Germain was exceptionally fluent in most of the great languages of Europe, the Middle East and Asian countries. His knowledge of ancient history was considered unparalleled among scholars, lending strong support to his assertion that he had been present at many of the most notable and world–shaking events of the historic past.

Several matters are certain about St. Germain. He possessed a superlative mastery of chemistry, far advanced for his time. It is acknowledged that he invented certain chemical dyes still in use today. Also, he was an accomplished musician. Audiences thrilled to his virtuosity on the violin. He was proficient in the area of musical compositions as well. His *Musique Raisonée* and *Seven Solos for a Violin* are still being played. A master at oil painting he was a genius at mixing oil pigments, and the famed painters Latour and Van Loo begged in vain for this secret.

One of the most remarkable aspects of St. Germain's life was his continual access to vast wealth. This was considered miraculous by his peers. St. Germain would closet himself in his secret laboratory and emerge after a time with impressive amounts of newly minted gold and silver coins. There would also be precious stones of astronomical value. In his *athanor*, an alchemical oven, St. Germain often repaired and "enlarged" jewels belonging to King Louis XV of France and his mistress, Madame Pompadour.

Beside all this, St. Germain was an astonishing healer, possessing a prodigious skill in the medical arts. There can be no doubt of his endless talents; it was as though he was endowed with all the knowledge handed down through the centuries. Plus knowledge that mankind did not have then and *still* does not have.

English author Horace Walpole (*The Castle of Otranto*) met St. Germain in London in 1743 and was deeply awed by the strange distinguished nobleman. While visiting that capital St. Germain aroused the "insatiable curiosity" of the Prince of Wales, who considered the Count a great genius.

At one time during his travels St. Germain met the famous writers, brothers Jacob and Wilhelm Grimm. They rated him as the most capable man they had ever met. The renowned Frederick the Great labelled the Count "one of the most enigmatic personages of the eighteenth century." In Casanova's memoirs St. Germain was called an impostor, although the jealous Casanova did rate him "the best he'd ever met." Cagliostro became a pupil of St. Germain and declared that his teacher was the Adept who founded modern Freemasonry. The lusty Catherine the Great, who was known to entertain whole regiments in her boudoir after fighting hours (one at a time of course), according to historical record appointed St. Germain a general in her army. There is no record of St. Germain's performance as a lover. But if his other talents are any indication, he must have been the highpoint of Catherine's love life.

Naturally it follows that St. Germain had psychic talents in abundance. Long before the French Revolution occurred, the Count publicly prophesied this event at a lavish party in Paris, much to the discomfort of the noble guests in attendance. In vain he sought to convince Louis XV to join the Rosicrucian Order and thus save his dynasty. Only days before the revolution began he journeyed to Paris to try to persuade Louis XVI and Marie Antoinette to quit the capital temporarily and save their lives, so they could return later to restore their throne. But they did not heed his warning, and St. Germain left Paris in despair. In Vienna he foresaw and detailed the rise of Napoleon Bonaparte. He also outlined his idea for a new type of ocean-going vessel he called a "steamship", that, he claimed, would forever alter commerce on the high seas.

St. Germain's fabulous knowledge and apparently unprecedented longevity alone would make him a prime candidate for vampirism. And his Longevity is pretty well established. Countess de Gergy, widow of the French ambassador to Italy,first met St. Germain in Venice in 1710. This was years before he appeared initially at the Royal Court in Versailles. When she encountered him a second time at the French Court some fifty years later, she wrote in her memoirs that he had scarcely changed at all. He looked about the same, she declared, still about forty five years of age. And this was *half a century after their first meeting*! The composer Rameau, by then quite old, insisted that he originally met St. Germain in 1701, and at that date *he was also forty-five years of age*.

It was Frederick the Great himself who finally settled the question when he publicly proclaimed that *"St. Germain could not Die!"*

Gossip had it that St. Germain really was The Wandering Jew of literature and legend. Many eighteenth century savants were convinced of this. St. Germain's extensive travels included visits to India (St. Germain stated that he accompanied Clive there in 1755), to Persia, Turkey, Japan and China. We can only guess at the other countries in his itinerary; he may even have journeyed to mystical Tibet. What was amazing about this man was his wide familiarity with life, with languages; with the customs of the people of these far flung nations. It is almost impossible to deny St. Germain's presence in these countries at one time or another. The question is not his talent for observation and learning, but whether an eighteenth century renaissance man could do so much within a normal life span.

The riddle of this big question mark fascinated the English writer, Sir Edward Bulwer-Lytton, author of *The Last Days of Pompeii* (1834). So involved did he become with the subject of St. Germain that Bulwer-Lytton made the count his immortal/Adept hero in his novel *Zanoni* (1842).

Even to this day, St. Germain's recorded longevity puzzles modern historians researching his life This aspect of his history obsessed the Czech playwright Karel Capek and inspired him to write *The Makropoulos Secret* (1923), a stunning drama about the key to immortality, subsequently turned into a twentieth century opera masterpiece by Leos Janacek.

Another tantalising connection to St. Germain was the French Madame de Genlis who collaborated on *Souvenirs* with the Countess d'Adhémar, an American. Both claimed to have met St. Germain in Vienna in 1821. In the purported biography of St. Germain, written in Vienna in 1845, he wrote that he offered the following prediction to the noted Austrian author, Franz Graffer:

"Toward the end of the century, I shall disappear out of Europe and betake myself to the Himalayas. Exactly in eighty-five years will people again set eyes on me. Farewell . . ."

If St. Germain is a man of his word, he is about to – or has - reappeared somewhere in the world. We will have to watch the newscasts closely for word of him.

However there may already have been appearances of the elusive count in the interim since he vanished at the close of nineteenth century. A 1910 Russian newspaper reported the brief visit in Siberia of a strange and mystical figure who was reluctant to identify himself. A letter found on his person was addressed to "Count Rakoczi". In 1925 Theosophist C. W. Leadbetter claims to have met unexpectedly with St. Germain in Rome. He describes the count as "looking like an ordinary Italian gentleman", of medium height, standing erect in a military manner. His hair, without the eighteenth century wig, was brown and close-cropped, centre parted in the fashion of the time. What impressed Leadbetter were the radiant eyes of this memorable man. They were large and brown, with a humourous twinkle in them and a sort of awesome sense of power.

During World War II, an American aviator crash-landed on the

Himalayas while he was ferrying supplies. In the snow-covered mountain wilderness where he came down, the pilot stumbled upon a solitary figure dressed in very odd, old fashioned European garments - hardly something a local native would use. This man introduced himself to the startled flyer as the Count of St. Germain, a name unfamiliar to the aviator. The extraordinary figure then advised the flyer on how to reach help, thus saving his life in the inhospitable area.

The pilot's written record of his strange adventure is still in the files of the U.S. Army.

In further search of the count, it has long been rumoured among *cognoscenti* in occult circles that the elusive and seemingly ageless figure of St. Germain resides today in a secret Carpathian Mountains retreat, in northern Hungary. Like the High Lama of Shangri-La in James Hilton's novel *Lost Horizon*, the Count is said to live in his mountain eyrie in strict privacy, receiving only a few select and privileged visitors whom he instructs in the mysteries of power and longevity.

Here perhaps is one of man's greatest mysteries. Who really was this mysterious historical figure? Many have tried without success to solve this enigma. Even Napoleon III (who ruled France from 1852 to 1870) set up a royal commission to resolve the questions about the life and times of the enigmatic count. But a puzzling fire of unknown origin at the Hotel de Ville destroyed all the irreplaceable documents relating to St. Germain that his officials had collected, ending that line of inquiry. In some circles it is believed that it was the Count himself who started the fire to protect his secret formulae from the eyes of the uninitiated.

As earlier stated, Ferenc Rakoczi, Count of St. Germain, in addition to his apparent immortality, was never observed to eat or drink. At public banquets he politely refused all sustenance, explaining that he had already "sustained himself previously *in his own manner.*" It was also noted that he shunned bright sunlight, going about at night or during overcast days.

St. Germain certainly possessed all the classic symptoms of the traditional vampire. One of history's great riddles awaits our solution. Was it all tongue in cheek? *Or teeth in neck?*

10. IN SEARCH OF DRACULA

A Personal Voyage

~ *Jonathan Barry* ~

I first became interested in Dracula when I was 14 years of age, having discovered a copy of the book in my parent's house. As I leafed through the foreword on the first page I was amazed to discover that Bram Stoker was an Irishman - not an American or English author - but a Dubliner. Not only this but he was born and raised in Clontarf, the same suburb where I had lived most of my life. I remember that this excited me greatly - that the author of one of the most famous novels in the world had started his life in the leafy suburb of Clontarf. I felt a sense of pride somehow, and was gripped with a fascination to find out more about him, and how he created such a fantastic monster. It was a fascination that would never leave me.

During my teenage years I also discovered that the vampire in Stoker's novel was based on a true-life person called Vlad Dracula, or Vlad the Impaler, who ruled as Prince of Wallachia (modern day Romania) between 1455-62. Vlad was famed for his cruelty and was described in his own lifetime in two 15th century documents as a "wampyr" (vampire), "stregoica" (witch), and as "ordog" and "pokol" (Satan and Hell)[1]. It was while working in London that Stoker himself first heard of Vlad through a meeting with Arminius Vambéry - A Hungarian traveller[2]. Vambéry met twice with Stoker, in 1890 and again in 1892, when it is believed that Vambéry introduced him to Vlad, providing him with the genesis for his novel. I wanted to know more about this Vlad Dracula, who he really was, how much Stoker had learnt of him, and how much influence he had on the vampire in the novel. I promised myself that one day I would go in search of this historical Dracula and visit Transylvania in Romania to see what remained of this terrible prince.

It was not until many years later when I was living and working in London that an opportunity arose for me to live out this dream. I was working at the time on an animated movie and an unexpected lull in production gave me time off to have an extended holiday. I had saved up enough money to go somewhere special and I began to nurture thoughts of a trip to Transylvania. It was May 1991 and I was living in Ealing in West London. I paid a visit to my local library which had a particularly good stock of travel guides and while browsing through the shelves I stumbled across a book called"Romanian Journey," by Andrew Mackenzie. The title caught my eye and as I examined the contents I spotted a chapter called "On the Dracula Trail."

The author it seems, like myself, was fascinated with the historical Vlad Dracula and had visited all the sites associated with him in Romania. To my great excitement I discovered that Dracula was buried in a tomb in a tiny monastery on an island in the middle of Lake Snagov, which lies not far outside Bucharest. None of the books I had read before about Dracula had ever mentioned this tomb and I was thrilled, however late, to discover its existence. I determined immediately to book a flight to Transylvania and to go that same week. As on all my travels, I packed my camcorder as I intended to make a video of my research.

I was quite nervous when the day arrived to board the plane to Bucharest, as the Ceaucescu revolution had erupted just one and a half years before and it was impossible to know what to expect. On arrival at Bucharest my fears seemed justified when passengers were greeted by heavily armed Romanian soldiers, signalling that all was not yet settled. As I passed through customs I noticed I was one of few Westerners on board the plane and I immediately felt awkward and self-conscious. Just as I was beginning to feel I had made a dreadful mistake, a smiling Romanian stepped forward and greeted me with a warm handshake. His name was Ion Pantelimonescu and he had been appointed by the travel agents in Bucharest to act as my driver to take me to and from my hotel.

I was relieved to step inside his car away from the peering eyes and I found Ion to be a warm, courteous and intelligent person with an excellent command of spoken English. He was curious to know why I was visiting Romania and I told him I was on a personal journey to discover the sites associated with Vlad Dracula. Ion explained to me that he worked as a taxi-driver but was once Romania's national sword-fencing champion and had been part of the Romanian Olympic sword-fencing team for ten years. I was impressed with his credentials and it soon dawned on me that meeting

Ion was a stroke of luck because he explained to me that his best friend Dan was a Romanian cameraman with a great interest in Dracula. Ion offered to get in touch with Dan the next day as he would be of great practical assistance in helping to shoot my video, and between both of them he was sure they could take me wherever I wanted to go.

I was stunned by such open hospitality and I trusted Ion implicitly although we had only just met. My trust was well founded and to this day I have remained good friends with him and we have continued to write to each other over the past six years. On reaching the hotel I thanked him and agreed to meet his friend the following morning. That night I thought again about MacKenzie's book which referred to three important sites for those on the trail of Dracula: Bran Castle, the city fortress of Tirgoviste, and the island of Snagov where Vlad was buried. I had only once seen a photo of Bran Castle, the castle which Stoker had used for his castle in the novel. This was the castle that most tourists visited when searching for Dracula as it is identical to the castle described in Chapters Two and Three of *Dracula*. But MacKenzie explained that Vlad had several residencies in Romania and Bran was only a summer residence where Vlad visited occasionally. It was not his royal seat. The latter was at Tirgoviste, a fortress city that he built to guard himself against the attacking Turks in the 15th century. It was from here that he launched his military campaigns against the Sultan's armies and where he committed some of his worst atrocities.

The next day I met Dan Alexandra, Ion's friend, and decided that it was best to visit Bran Castle first as it was a three hour drive through the Carpathian Mountains, and by far the longest of the three journeys. As we drove through the suburbs of Bucharest I was saddened at the destruction of the city caused by Ceaucescu's building programs, all of which were abandoned following his execution. The People's Palace lay empty and whole streets of half-built tower blocks were scattered across the skyline. It looked more like a bomb site from World War II than a thriving modern capital.

I was glad when we left the city and started our approach to the Carpathians. I had no idea that the Carpathians were one of the largest mountain ranges in Eastern Europe, running in backbone fashion across hundreds of miles of Romanian countryside. The description of the Carpathians in the novel was identical to what was unfolding before my eyes - vast swaths of coniferous and deciduous woodland, completely

Bran Castle, Transylvania, Romania –
identical to the castle described in Chapters 2 and 3 of *Dracula*.

unspoilt, encroaching from every side of the road and rising thousands of feet amongst snow-capped mountains. Dan told me that the Carpathians were still home to wolves and bears which roamed freely as common as foxes in Ireland. While wolves were driven from Western and Central Europe by the end of the 19th century the Carpathians remained one of their last great refuges in the world.

As we drove I told Dan that I was amazed how little the Carpathians seemed to have changed since Vlad's time, and he explained that this was because of a lack of industrialisation under Ceaucescu's communist regime.

After what seemed like an age the road suddenly began to descend and I saw Bran Castle before me, perched on an enormous rock in the most dramatic of settings. A thrill of excitement ran through me as it raised its head above the trees in an almost threatening fashion. When we reached the entrance of the castle I was amazed at Stoker's accuracy. In Chapter Three of "Dracula" he says:

> The castle was built on the corner of a great rock, so that on three sides it was quite impregnable, and great windows were placed here where sling, or bow, or culverin could not reach, and consequently light and comfort, impossible to a position which had to be guarded, were secured. To the West was a great valley, and then, rising far away, great jagged mountain fastnesses, rising peak on peak, the sheer rock studded with mountain ash and thorn, whose roots clung in cracks and crevices and crannies of the stone.[3]

I stood at the base of Bran Castle and read this passage aloud to the camera to demonstrate to Dan the perfect accuracy of Stoker's description, even down to the mountain ash and thorn, which to this day still surround the base of the castle. It is more incredible when we realise that Stoker never went to Transylvania and never saw Bran Castle at all! So where did he get his information? In his book *Vampyres*, Christopher Frayling explains that Stoker derived much of his information from several travel guides of the 19th century, including *Transylvania*, by Charles Boner which was published in 1865, and *On the Track of the Crescent*, by Major E.C. Johnson, published in 1885[4]. Both books had pull-out maps and contained vivid descriptions of the Carpathians and the castles found there.

As we entered the castle courtyard I was dismayed to see that the castle was closed due to extensive renovation work. Dan had not expected this, but with a small bribe of several hundred Lei (Romanian currency) I managed to persuade the solitary caretaker to let me into the castle with my camcorder. The interior of the castle was again identical to that described in the novel, with numerous turrets, low ceilings, spiral staircases, hexagonal and octagonal shaped rooms, dark and winding passageways and a terrible sense of gloom and isolation. Heavy wooden doors black with age led from chamber to chamber, and in one room I noticed a peculiar black opening in the furthest corner of the room. Curious to find out what it was, I approached it to find three tiny spiral steps leading into a hole in the wall which was black with darkness.

Sticking my head and camera into the dark opening I found a passageway leading to the upper ramparts of the castle.

Vlad Tepes – impalement was his favourite method of execution

It was barely the width of a person and was pitch black except for a dull grey gap of light at what must have been the other end. It was frightening even at this hour of the day and on my own I did not have the nerve to enter the passageway to see where it led. It was simply too dark. It reminded me of the passageway which Dracula used in the novel which led to the enclosed bed chamber of Jonathan Harker which could not be locked from the inside. While I pondered what to do I heard the caretaker approaching and she told me it was time to leave. Thus ended my visit to the castle. As we left the premises I sensed indeed that this was a sinister place and the remoteness of the castle would linger long in my memory.

The following day Ion kindly offered to take me to Tirgoviste, the fortress city where Vlad had ruled. The journey there was a simpler one, avoiding the Carpathians and travelling through a flat and monotonous landscape until we reached the town. At the centre of the town on a busy thoroughfare we found the remains of the fortress. Unlike Bran Castle which was remarkably well preserved, many of the walls at Tirgoviste had fallen away to reveal the hulks of broken battlements. However, the entrance to the fortress was still standing, crowned by a hexagonal tiled turret peculiar to Romanian architecture. As we passed under its archway Ion pointed to a plaque inset on the wall. It was a list of all the Princes who had ruled at Tirgoviste when it held power and sway over most of Romania in the 15th century. Reading through the names on the plaque, two in particular stood out from the rest, those of Vlad Dracul, and directly below it, Vlad Tepes.

This confused me slightly until Ion explained to me that Vlad Dracul was the uncle of Vlad Dracula and had reigned before him. Vlad Tepes was the name the Turks used when they referred to Vlad Dracula (Tepes meaning "impaler"). So he had three names: Vlad Dracula which he was christened, Vlad Tepes the name given him by the Turks, and Vlad the Impaler, a name given him by Western historians for obvious reasons.

As we passed through the archway the solid figure of a round stone tower emerged before us and I instantly recognised it as Chindia Tower - a prison house where Vlad had tortured many of his victims. In his book, *Romanian Journey*, MacKenzie had mentioned this tower as an important link-up between the historical Dracula and the vampire in the novel. The tower, he said, was now a Dracula Museum containing several important documents relating to Dracula, including the only known surviving document signed by Dracula himself. Another vital document was a report written by the Papal Legate Nicholas Modrussa, who was sent by the Pope to interview Dracula while he was held captive for twelve years in Brasov by King Matthias Corvinus. It is the only description of Vlad passed down to us by history and it reads as follows:

> He was not very tall but very stocky and strong, with a cold and terrible appearance, a strong and aquiline nose, swollen nostrils, a thin and reddish face, in which very long eyelashes framed large wide-opened green eyes; the bushy black eyebrows made them appear threatening. His face and chin were shaven, but for a moustache. The swollen temples increased the bulk of his head. A bull's neck connected his head to his body from which black curly locks hung on his wide shouldered person.[5]

There is a marked similarity between this description and the description of the vampire in the novel. In Chapter Two of *Dracula*, Harker says:

> His face was a strong - a very strong - aquiline, with high bridge of the thin nose and peculiarly arched nostrils; with lofty domed forehead, and hair growing scantily round the temples, but profusely elsewhere. His eyebrows were very massive, almost meeting over the nose, and with bushy hair that seemed to curl in its own profusion. The mouth, so far as I could see it under the heavy moustache, was fixed and rather cruel-looking.[6]

The coincidences here are too strong and it demonstrates that Stoker must have read this papal document during his research hours either at the British Museum or at Whitby. To my great annoyance Chindia Tower was closed that day and this time there was no one around that could be bribed to let me gain entrance to it. Frustrated, I had to accept that I would not see any of the Dracula documents that day and settled instead for a visit to his Basilica which was built beside it. It was ironic that he built a house of torture and a house of worship side by side. The walls of the Basilica were covered in detailed medieval frescoes and its pillars in gold mosaics. The gilt from the gold had faded to an imperceptible muddy brown with many of the portraits depicted on the pillars barely distinguishable. Dracula had built the Basilica himself and all that remained of him was his black ebony throne where he sat in attendance at mass almost every day.

It was hard for me to believe that this was the same man, who after the Battle of Tirgau, marched 20,000 Turks to Tirgoviste where he impaled them outside the city walls along with the remains of 6,000 boyars

(Romanian nobility) whom he had impaled six weeks earlier. It was a sobering thought and one which made me shudder. Overall the trip to Tirgoviste was a disappointment and as we left the battlements we saw outside what remained of the forest that Vlad had felled to impale the 20,000 Turks. 20,000 trees is a lot of wood!

The last leg of our journey still remained, and later that week we set out for Dracula's tomb, a journey which would be the highlight of my trip. It had been raining hard during my stay in Bucharest and the day we set out for Snagov was no exception. The lake where Dracula was buried was at the heart of a dense and ancient woodland which spread for miles on its perimeter. Ion knew the woodland and its environs well, explaining to me that while he was part of the Romanian Olympic team they had trained at a hidden base on the banks of Lake Snagov. At that time the lake and its surrounding woodlands were directly under Ceaucescu's control as it was home to one of his numerous palace residencies. But since his execution the lake and its forests were now in public domain. As we penetrated deeper into Ceaucescu's former estate we passed through numerous sentry posts abandoned to the elements.

At a certain point as we closed in on the lakeshore, the road became a

I bought this rare postcard from one of the three monks who live on the island of Snagov — which is 23 miles outside Bucharest in Romania.

The three monks guard and protect the tomb of Vlad Dracula (the Impaler) inside the church at the monastery. After seeing Dracula's tomb I bought

this postcard from the Father as a memory of the occasion.

Jonathan Barry
2nd June 1991.

MÎNĂSTIREA SNAGOV – monument istoric
de arhitectură (sec. XIV)
1. Dreptul Judecător (icoană sec. XVIII).
2. Vedere generală dinspre lac.
3. Icoana Maicii Domnului (sec. XVIII).
4. Biserica Mînăstirii.
5. Tabloul votiv.
6. Vlad Țepeș, ctitorul principal al așezării

dirt track. We ploughed through the flooded track and thick mud. Eventually a clearing in the trees appeared and I got my first sight of the tiny island which lay less than a quarter of a mile from the lakeside. Four spiked turrets stood out clearly above the treetops and Ion said we would have to walk the rest of the way to get closer to the edge of the lake. One of Ion's friends had told him of a local woman living on the lakeside who, twice a day, rowed to the monastery to sell her eggs to the monks. She was the only person with direct daily contact with the monastery and was our best hope of getting to the island.

Ion located her cottage and he explained to the woman that I had come a long way to visit Dracula's tomb and could she ask the monks if I could visit the island. With a big smile and typical Romanian courtesy she said she would row to the island and ask the monks - but could not be sure of their response. They had become fearful of anyone visiting the island since the Ceaucescu revolt and viewed all persons with suspicion. It was a nail-biting twenty minutes as we saw her row to the island and speak to the lone figure of the Father of the monastery. Ion shouted across to interpret for the Father so that he clearly understood I was no government spy. I was terribly nervous having come so far that I might be turned away.

At last we saw the boat returning with the stocky woman rowing in earnest. Ion shouted to her and translated to me that they had agreed to let me visit. I was thrilled with excitement that a lifetime's ambition was about to be realised. As the boat pulled into the slip we stepped in gingerly and joined the woman and her black Labrador puppy. I thanked her profusely and offered to pay her for her efforts but she refused to take anything. There was a beautiful calm on the lake with dozens of swifts and swallows circling the boat as they dived between the hidden turrets of the monastery and the reeds of the lakeshore. The woman explained that there were only three monks on the island including the Father and it had remained a tiny congregation since the 13th century. The monks had guarded Dracula's tomb since his defeat at Snagov in 1462 when he was beheaded and his body laid to rest in the monastery.

Within minutes we pulled up by the simple wooden jetty that connected the monastery to the outside world. My heart was pounding as we stepped out onto the mooring and were approached by the striking dark figure of the Father. He was dressed from head to toe in the traditional black outfit of the Romanian Orthodox Church, which is identical in appearance to the dress of the Russian Orthodox Church - a long black tunic, split black beard, and black mitre. To an outside observer he could easily have passed as a priest from the time of the Tzars, so antiquated was his appearance.

He instructed us to wait as he went to open the chapel where Vlad was buried. The chapel itself was a small building of red clay bricks capped by two hexagonal turrets on an almost flat roof. The entrance was comprised of two panelled doors black from discolouration which opened from the outside in. As the Father turned the key the doors swung inwards revealing a total darkness. As we entered the light seemed to follow our footsteps because once inside we could clearly see the medieval artifacts before us. Like the Basilica in Tirgoviste the walls and pillars were covered in an array of medieval icons depicting the Madonna, Jesus and all the Apostles. A heavy brass chandelier hung from a vaulted ceiling supported by a massive chain. A wonderful smell of decay and history permeated the air.

Through a pulled curtain we entered the inner chamber and at last I saw the tomb I thought I would never see. It lay sunken in the floor before me, an unassuming simple slab of grey stone surrounded by a thin rectangular border of white marble - similar in many ways to the white surround of modern graves. Across its length lay a thin rug of red, white and black stripes with small red tassels on either end. A tiny vase stood at one end of the rug, and a print of his famous portrait at the other end. I stood in awe, both at having reached the tomb and knowing who was laid inside it. I contemplated the mystery and legend that surrounded him and although I knew his remains were all but gone I felt a sense of personal contact in the quiet solitude of the tiny chapel. Vlad Dracula lay beneath my feet and I wondered what Bram Stoker would have felt had he too stood in this position.

After some minutes the Father entered and kindly offered me a bag of incense as a souvenir of my visit to the tomb. I thanked him and to this day still have the bag in my possession. It was too precious to burn and when I smell it now it reminds me of that day in Snagov. It was a small token but one which I appreciated. Once outside the Father translated through Ion to tell me that I was the first Westerner since the Ceaucescu revolt of December 1989 to reach Dracula's tomb - this mainly because political unrest had kept most Westerners away. I was amazed to hear this and it made my visit all the more special.

I thanked the Father for his kindness and took one last look back at the chapel as we stepped into the boat once more. A real sense of pride and achievement filled my veins that I had lived out my dream in a land where I had expected the worst - but had received the best. Luck played a good part of it admittedly, but the determination had always been there without which it would never have happened. It was a journey I shall never forget and one which I shall cherish for the rest of my life.

FOOTNOTES

1 Ludlum, Harry (1962).
   A Biography of Dracula   London: W. Foulsham & Co
                                                      p.100.

2 Stoker, Bram (1906).
   Personal Reminiscences of Henry Irving, 2 Volumes London: W. Heinemann.
                                                      pp.371-372.

3 Stoker, Bram (1993).
   Dracula   London: Penguin Classics.
                                                      p.50.

4 Frayling, Christopher (1991).
   Vampyres   London: Faber & Faber.
                                                      pp.317-346.

5 MacKenzie, Andrew.(1983).
   Romanian Journey   London: Robert Hale.
                                                      p.138.

6 Stoker, Bram (1993).
   Dracula   London: Penguin Classics.
                                                      p.28.

11. DRACULA AND ME

~ *Don Conroy* ~

We sat huddled in the darkness, my brother Séamus and me. I have my overcoat wrapped around me like a blanket, peering over the collar, staring with terror and fascination at the screen. I was not the only one. Teenage girls hugged boyfriends tightly. Any moment he would appear. Who was his next victim to be? Then several loud shrieks warned us that he was out there beyond the house, lurking in the shadows like a predator ready to pounce on some hapless victim. I ducked down below the seat.

'Sit still!' my older brother snapped. Then the Count appeared, eyes blood-shot, lips spreading to reveal the deadly fangs. His black cape like a shroud cloaking him with the darkness. How could my brother not be scared, I wondered. But his hands gripping the wooden arm rests revealed his tension. There was an irresistible impulse in one to see what would happen next, despite one's fears.

When the curtain finally came down in the Sandford Cinema on that Friday evening's show of the 'Horror of Dracula', I thanked God for Van Helsing who put an end to my fears. Only to find they began to surface again as we walked from Ranelagh to Donnybrook and the darkness creeping in on that summer evening .

Eddie, my brother's pal who came with us to the cinema said to me: 'You're such a baby. It wasn't creepy at all.'

My brother half agreed but admitted it had its frightening moments.

As we walked on home a man moved out from the shadows of a laneway. Well you have never seen three children move as fast as we raced down the road to the safety of our homes. A rosary beads was hung on the bed post before we went to bed just in case we had any unwelcome midnight callers. Thankfully my brother and I were sharing the same bedroom.

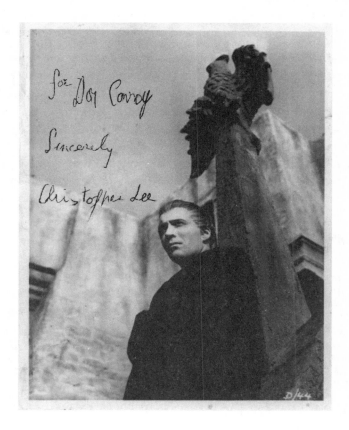

After scolding my brother for bringing me to a scary movie like that, my mother later explained 'Dracula' was only an actor dressed up to look like a vampire. My sister Tina picked up on this and suggested I should write to Christopher Lee and ask him for his autograph. Eventually in my best nine-year-old handwriting I wrote to: Christopher Lee c/o Hammer Films, England.

To my amazement I received a response. Not only an autograph, but a picture of Mr Lee dressed in his Dracula clothes, cape and all. I still have the photograph, a prized possession for any movie buff like myself.

* * *

Whether from the literary or visual world, horror or fantasy has never lost its hold on the imagination. As science continues to answer so many questions about life and the world about us, the imagination seems to be retreating to the margins, like some wolf at the edge of extinction.

The over-mechanized world can at times be a rather colourless world in which to live. This may be the reason why people still yearn for the fancied worlds of their imagination. Much superstition and folklore have fallen victim to the cold logic of science. But the down side of science with its death machines and pollution of the planet is all too familiar to us through the medium of television and print. We are constantly reminded of the real horrors that have eclipsed any vampire, werewolf or zombie, that may roam the nights of our dreams. They at least preserve the semblance of human form, unlike the spectre of nuclear destruction or other such grim reaper we have to live with.

We don't need science to tell us vampires, werewolves, ghosts or Frankenstein monsters don't exist. For we do know they exist in the fertile imagination of writers and artists. In the safety of a good book we can be transported to the Carpathian Mountains where the Count resides, or be with a mad scientist as he creates his hideous monster, listen to the frightening drums as the voodoo ceremony gets underway on an island of the West Indies. Or hurry down the dimly lit, foggy alleys of Victorian London in pursuit of the deadly Mr Hyde. We have nothing to fear, for we know they are all figments of the world of imagination.

But before we put out the lights, let us check we have a crucifix or a wooden stake by our bedside just in case!

12. CHURCHILL TALKS TO STOKER

Stoker as a journalist
~ Bram Stoker ~

Bram Stoker was acquainted with Winston Spencer Churchill (one of the earliest admirers of *Dracula*) for nearly twenty-five years. Not long before Churchill married in 1908 (Bram and Florence were guests at the wedding), this fascinating article was published in *The Daily Chronicle* (15 January 1908).

Throughout his long and unique political career Churchill hated giving interviews to anyone, so this interview was quite a scoop for Bram Stoker – mainly brought about by Churchill's great liking for *Dracula*!

The Daily Chronicle
Wednesday, January 15, 1908

Mr Winston Churchill
talks of his hopes, his work, and his ideals,
to Bram Stoker.

(On the eve of the return to England of Mr. Winston Churchill after an African tour extending from British East Africa to the Nile, the following sketch by Mr. Bram Stoker of one of the most striking personalities in political life will be read with interest).

When I wrote to Mr. Winston Churchill asking for an appointment to interview him he replied: "I would very much rather not; but if you wish it, I cannot refuse you." When I met him in his library he explained more fully in words:

"I hate being interviewed, and I have refused altogether to allow it. But I have to break the rule for you, for you were a friend of my father." Then he added gracefully another reason, personal to myself: "And because you are the author of *Dracula*." This latter was a vampire novel I wrote some years ago, which had appealed to his young imagination. He had himself been an imaginative writer. The first thing of his which I remember reading was a powerful short story called "Man Overboard", a grim, striking story wherein he followed the last thoughts of a drowning man.

As he had already written, some ten years ago, *Savrola*, a political novel, I asked him if he intended or wished to write others, in case he should have time to do so through the revolutions of the political wheel. He answered thoughtfully: "No, I think not; not novels. I hope to write, and to write as much as public life will give me opportunity of doing. But I do not think it will be fiction."

"I would rather write something in the lighter forms of history - a sort of truthful story-telling. It seems to me that the whole tendency of modern historical research is to subdivide and prosecute investigation into each division or aspect of the matter separately. It is all done by sections. The result is not satisfactory. We used to have less details but a general picture, whereas now we get superabundant details but no general sketch, no picture or story. The work should neither be of too great length, nor should it be written for children. There is a growing opportunity for writers who will grip a subject as a whole and convey it intelligently to the plain man who wants to know but hasn't got much time. The popularity of Pitchett's book of *Deeds That Won The Empire* illustrates what I mean."

~~~~~~~~~~~~~~~~~~~~~~~~

£25
**Twenty-five pounds sterling REWARD
is offered by the Sub-Commission of the
Fifth Division, on behalf of the Special
Constable of the said division to anyone
who brings the escaped prisoner of war,**

CHURCHILL,
**living or dead to this office.
For the Sub-Commission of the Fifth
Division. LODK DE HAAS, Secretary.**

~~~~~~~~~~~~~~~~~~~~~~~~

The 'Reward' poster, printed on poor paper in rough type, somewhat after the manner of hue-and-cry placards for runaway niggers in the bad times of slavery, was the notice which followed the escape of Winston Spencer Churchill, war correspondent, from the prison at the Model School in Pretoria in December 1899.

Seven years later the Transvaal was a British Colony, and the ex-prisoner, Winston Churchill, was Under Secretary for the Colonies in the British Government; an Under Secretary who manifestly had, and who was manifestly intended to have, an important share in the formation of the new Constitution of the new British Colony. "Thus", says Feste, the jester, "the whirligigs of time brings in his revenges."

I found Mr. Winston Churchill in his study at his pretty house in Bolton Street, off Piccadilly. The Under Secretary of the Colonies is a working man and a bachelor; the whole of the first floor usually allotted domestically for a drawing-room is here utilised as a study, two rooms having been thrown into one. The houses in this part of Bolton Street are not large, and in them every inch of space is generally arranged by clever architects to practical use. The colour tone of the room is rich green, relieved somewhat gloomily by the heavy mahogany panelling and the many bookcases of the same dark wood, velvet pile carpet of green, green chairs and sofas.

The study table is a somewhat remarkable one: an immensely large and wide piece of Chippendale in mahogny with carved legs and bevelled edges richly carved; a table that seems as though it were made for the work of collating documents. Elsewhere in the double room are pretty pieces of Empire furniture of tulip-wood.

The shelves are filled with a varied assortment of books, mostly editions de luxe, showing the catholic taste of the Churchill family, for very many of these editions have the book plate of Lord Randolph Churchill. Here in addition to the heavier works of history, philosophy and those bearing on politics and public life, are fine editions handsomely bound of Edgar Allan Poe, Carlyle, Richardson, Jane Austen, Dean Milman, George Grote, the Brontes, etc.

Of course there are not here the accumulations of letters and papers; of Blue-Books and files of documents which cumber up a statesman's office. All such are in his rooms at the Colonial Office and the House of Commons. Though a Minister may - and does - do much of his work in his own home, the work of this class is selected, and only such papers and authorities as are required are brought to him.

Over the fireplace in the outer room is set in the panel a fine portrait by Romney of an officer, Captain Peletan, in uniform. The windows are double framed so that the war of the elements and the roar of traffic in the neighbouring Piccadilly can be effectually kept out. On the wall of the inner room, set so as to face one, is a lifelike portrait of the Right Hon. Lord Randolph Churchill.

When I came to London to be Henry Irving's manager, my acquaintance with Lord Randolph Churchill, made in Ireland, continued. Our relations were always most friendly. He often came to the Lyceum Theatre; he was a great admirer of Irving, and occasionally stayed for supper in the old Beefsteak Room.

One evening at the theatre - I think it was during the long run of 'Faust' - when between the acts I was walking in the passage, I heard his voice behind me:

"Oh, Bram Stoker, I want to introduce my boy to you." I turned, and the introduction was made. Young Winston was then about thirteen, a strongly-built boy with red hair and very red cheeks. A bright-looking boy, somewhat on the sturdy side, and eminently healthy. As we shook hands the father laid his hand affectionately on the boy's shoulder, and, patting it in a loving way, said:

"He's not much yet, you know. But he's a good 'un. He's a good 'un!" and a "good 'un" he turned out to be.

The son has more than fulfiled the predictions of the father. He is at this moment in the foremost rank of living British statesmen, his dashing, pugnacious methods allied to his great gifts as a speaker, his lucid power in handling public questions, and his remarkable breadth of view, distinguishing him above all his rivals.

"Why," I asked him, presently, "did you leave the army? You seem to have liked soldiering and to have got on very well with it."

"I was very happy in the Army. I did like soldiering. But the fact is that in peace time there is little if any scope in the army for a man who wants to be active. Of course, I mean very active, and in different ways, for there is always plenty of routine work in military service. anyhow, a man must choose his own way of life, and if it is only fighting that a man wants there is plenty of that in politics. It is only by following out one's own bent that there can be the really harmonious life."

"Won't you define," I asked, "what you mean exactly by that?" He smiled. I do not think that he cares much for definitions; he makes up his mind in his own way, a way to satisfy himself.

"Harmonious life. A life when a man's work is also his pleasure and vice versa. That conjunction, joined with a buoyant temperament, makes the best of worldly gifts."

"Why buoyant temperament? I merely ask for information."

"Simply because it implies a lot of other things: good health and strength, for instance. The great majority of human beings have to work the greater part of the day, and then amuse themselves afterwards - if they are not too tired. But the lucky few derive their keenest interest and enjoyment not from any contrast between business and idle hours - but from the work itself. But certainly physical health has a good deal to do with it. Henry James speaks of a religion of healthy usefulness."

"I note, Mr. Churchill," I said, "that you use the words politics and politician where I mean statesmanship and statesman. May I take it that I am in accord with your ideas?" There was a smile on his face as he answered:

"Don't you think it would be at least unbecoming of a man to speak of himself as a statesman? Politics and politician seem to me to be very good and adequate words, quite equal to the purpose required of them. Politics are quite big enough, I assure you."

"What, in your opinion, Is the modern tendency of politics?"

"All politics in this country, and I think all over the world, are becoming divided along social and economic lines of cleavage. The movements of the past have never so operated. The Reformation secured, directly and indirectly, freedom of conscience. The English revolution and rebellion of the seventeenth century established Parliamentary government. The French Revolution achieved a very considerable measure of political equality - the idea of a national nation - citizens not separated by class prejudice; but there yet remains the greatest of all the anomalies, the social and economic injustice. All politics are focussing on this."

"Perhaps it is for America to show the way. There is the naked issue between capital and labour. America's contribution to the movement for human progress will be some solution, necessarily complicated, of the economic problems which confront scientific civilisation."

The smile was not existent at the end of this guess at the future. Instead, there was a look of concentrated gravity - of deep, earnest purpose, which showed something of the man within. Behind the face-mask of boyhood there came something quite different - the something which revealed a passionate earnestness not to be suspected from his general appearance. The incipient wrinkles which only show occasionally on the smooth skin of his forehead seemed to deepen, the fine lines of the well-cut mouth to harden; the eyes to get a new and earnest look.

Winston Churchill is in his 34th year, with a record of four campaigns behind him and enough memories of personal adventures to equip a Ballantine or a Kingston. He has sat in Parliament for years and always as one of the most strenuous and daring of members. He has borne officially the heat of the day in the new Parliament which came into the turmoil after a reign of twenty years by their political opponents. In the Commons he has been the official mouthpiece of his party and Cabinet in Colonial matters, and has held himself worthily against all odds. But in appearance he is still a boy. Let us see him as he leans against the mantelpiece in his study, seemingly gay and debonair.

Of medium height, looking rather slimmer than he is, for he is compactly built. The red hair of his boyhood has lost some of its fire, and seems now rather a reddish brown than red. The eyes of light blue are large of pupil, having in them something of the free quality of the eyes of a bird. The mouth is an orator's mouth; clear cut, expressionable, and not small. The forehead is both broad and high, with a fairly deep vertical line above the nose; the chin strong and well formed. His hands are somewhat remarkable; a sort of index to his life as well as to his general character. They are distinctly strong hands. Broad in the palm, with that breadth which palmists take as showing honesty; fingers both long and fairly thick, but tapering; the thumb slightly bent backward at the top point. The man with such a hand should go far.

When I asked him to enlighten me as to his change of party he smiled again, but with a different one this time. It was a somewhat inscrutable smile, old wisdom looking out of the gleeful face of boyhood. He will, I think, take perennial delight in all that led up to that change and in the doing of it. His words, together with the tone in which they were spoken and that enlightening something which is conveyed by appearance, expression and manner all in unison, seemed to satisfy one's intellect.

"When I was in the Conservative Party, to which I had been brought up, I was called a Tory Democrat. Even then I belonged to the progressive wing of the party. I came into Parliament after the Boer War as a representative of the high-water mark of Tory Imperialism. But I was actually already in complete reaction against it. Indeed, I may say that when my change of party came there was not far to go. I went into politics on the Conservative side, just as a man might go to Oxford because his father had been there. My father was a Tory Democrat, and I had been brought up in that atmosphere.

"What is Tory Democracy?"

"The association of us all through the leadership of the past - that was what I thought it meant. It was only later on that I learned that its aspirations were exploited by the vested interests of Conservatism, simply to win the votes and popularity of working men."

"As he spoke my mind went back to a passage of his speech before the National Liberal Federation in Manchester in 1904 which seemed to link his old political faith with his new:

"We are here to sweep away the whisperings of despair. We are not going back; we are going on. Our movements are towards a better, fairer organisation of society, and our faith is strong and high that the time shall surely come - and will come the sooner for our efforts - when the dull, grey clouds under which millions of our countrymen are monotonously toiling will break and melt and vanish for ever in the sunshine of a new and noble age."

13. BRAM STOKER AND THE CINEMA

~ *Leslie Shepard* ~

In 1993 the release of Francis Ford Coppola's movie *Bram Stoker's Dracula* revived interest in a much neglected Irishman and his sensational novel, which has inspired hundreds of movies. Yet Stoker was essentially a man of the theatre and had no interest in the primitive peepshows and simple actualities of cinema at the time he was preparing his book. Like his father, Stoker was an avid theatre-goer, and was fascinated by the cultural and artistic achievements of the stage. He was also sufficiently overwhelmed by the performances of the great actor Henry Irving to devote twenty-seven years of his life to being Irving's manager.

Stoker wrote novels in his spare time from his more important work in the theatre, and would have been astounded by the proliferation of Dracula films over the last seventy years. He would surely have approved the standard stage play version of *Dracula* by Hamilton Deane, since he had arranged a rudimentary play reading of *Dracula* at the Royal Lyceum Theatre in London in 1897, to protect his stage copyright. But Hamilton Deane's play did not have an opening night until 1927, fifteen years after Stoker's death.

Only a few years earlier in 1921, a film based on Stoker's novel was first produced, launching an endless stream of *Dracula* and vampire movies. This was *Drakula*, a Hungarian film directed by Karoly Lajthay. So far as I know, this is a lost film.

A year later in 1922, came the most famous film version of Stoker's book. This was *Nosferatu, Eine Symphonie des Grauens* (*Nosferatu, A Symphony of Shadows*), directed by F.W. Murnau, a brilliant German director. This was also in danger of becoming a lost film, since in 1925, Florence, Stoker's widow, succeeded in obtaining an injunction against the film for infringement of copyright. All copies and the negative were ordered to be destroyed. Fortunately some copies escaped this fate. Murnau had hoped to avoid copyright problems by changing the names of the characters and also the locales; thus, Count Dracula became Count Orlock, Harker was Hutter, Renfield became Knock. Instead of Whitby in Britain, the Count came to Bremen in Germany. For many years surreptitious copies of the proscribed film circulated in the U.S.A., but it was not until 1984 that a fully restored version, as originally tinted, was shown after nine years work by Enno Patalas of the Munich Film Museum, using copies from as far afield as Switzerland, France and East Germany.

Meanwhile in 1930, Waldemar Rongar persuaded Murnau to collaborate on a new version of *Nosferatu*, involving some additional shooting, dubbing of dialogue, and yet another renaming of the characters to avoid copyright prosecution. Count Orlok was now Furst Wolkoff, Hutter (Jonathan Harker) became Kundberg, his wife Ellen became Margitta. This version, entitled *Die Zwolfe Stunde (The Twelfth Hour)*, was also revived by Enno Patalas in 1984, but I have not so far been able to see it or trace a copy.

Poster for *Dracula* (1931)
starring Bella Lugosi

In 1931, came the first Hollywood *Dracula*, directed by Tod Browning and starring Bela Lugosi as the Count. Interestingly enough, Browning had not favoured Lugosi for the part, suggesting Lon Chaney, but Chaney died before the film was cast. Other possibilities considered were Paul Muni and Conrad Veidt - the latter suggestion being of piquant interest, since Veidt had actually played in a film with Lugosi - the silent Jekyll and Hyde film titled *Der Januskopf* (1920), directed by F.W. Murnau, who went on to make the classic *Nosferatu* two years later. However, Bela Lugosi had already established himself in the role of Dracula in innumerable stage productions of the Hamilton Deane play, on which the Tod Browning picture was based.

This 1931 *Dracula* now seems intolerably slow and theatrical, but it was a landmark in the proliferation of Dracula films, launching the first great chapter of vampire and monster movies by the production company Universal. The great success of this movie encouraged Universal to try another monster movie. This was *Frankenstein*. Lugosi was offered the part of the Monster, but turned it down. He had now become identified with the role of Dracula, but unfortunately never mellowed his portentous stagey style of acting. The Monster was eventually played by Boris Karloff, a far more expressive film actor than Lugosi, who now found himself obliged to act in undistinguished "B" pictures on horror subjects. After a breakdown in health which required medication by morphine, Lugosi became a drug addict, even sleeping in a coffin. He died on 18th August 1956. Sixteen years later, his obsession with the part of Dracula was marked posthumously by a legal decision in Los Angeles in the case of *Lugosi et al v. Universal Pictures Company Inc., et al* in which the Superior Court in California held that the heirs of Bela Lugosi had an enforceable 'right of publicity' in Lugosi's name, his face and his characterisations.

After the success of the 1931 *Dracula*, Tod Browning went on to direct *Mark of the Vampire* for M.G.M. in 1935. Meanwhile in 1936, Universal released *Dracula's Daughter* (directed by Lambert Hillyer) as a sequel to *Dracula*, said to be based on the story *Dracula's Guest*, which was a chapter of *Dracula* omitted by Stoker in his final text, and later published separately as a short story.

After *Dracula's Daughter*, Universal released *Son of Dracula* in 1943, directed by Robert Siodmak, in which Count Alucard (an obvious anagram) was a nobleman from Transylvania, a part played by Lon Chaney Junior. Although the 'Alucard' name was later used again in another film, this concluded Universal's 'family descent' of Dracula, and we were mercifully spared a Dracula's Brother, Wife, or even Father and Mother prequels. But the success of other monster movie characters like *Frankenstein* and the *Wolf Man* suggested that it might be even more successful to put these characters together in films. In 1943, Universal had issued *Frankenstein Meets the Wolf Man*, and when this did well at the box office they launched a three-for-the-price-of-one movie *House of Frankenstein* in the following year, directed by Erle C. Kenton, featuring Boris Karloff, Lon Chaney, and John Carradine as the Count.

One trade paper commented : *"House of Frankenstein comes very close to being the horror picture to end all horror pictures"* - and it certainly seems that Universal planned this as the last of a series. All the leading characters were clearly killed off : Count Dracula was trapped by the rays of the rising sun (a hazard which had first appeared in Murnau's 1922 *Nosferatu*, but was later discarded in other horror films); the Wolf Man was shot by a silver bullet, and the Frankenstein Monster and the mad scientist were swallowed by a quicksand. However, in the following year, Universal had second thoughts, and offered *House of Dracula*, also directed by Erle C. Kenton, with Carradine repeating his role as Dracula, and Lon Chaney as the Wolf Man. This was a surprisingly short feature of only 67 minutes in length.

No explanations were offered for the miraculous reappearance of the main characters after their earlier apparently irreversible deaths. And in this sequel, Dracula himself once again perishes by sunlight when his casket is opened in broad daylight - surely an illogical convention, since few vampires would be able to organise absolutely light-proof vaults. A trade paper also raised another practical plot difficulty: "The literal minded in the audiences may still be disturbed by one point, however. Who does his laundry? His shirt front remains immaculately white after those many hours spent lying in coffins-full of his native soil. Obviously it is laundered. But how?"

In 1946, Universal reorganised as Universal-International and announced another several-for-the-price-of-one monster movie: *The Brain of Frankenstein*, but this time, the stock monsters Count Dracula, The Wolf Man and Frankenstein's Monster were to be joined by Count Alucard (from the earlier *Son of Dracula*) and even Kharis the Mummy. However, the scriptwriting team managed to eliminate the Mummy and Count Alucard, and after many script conferences the picture finally went into production as *Abbott and Costello Meet Frankenstein*, released in 1948. But this time, Dracula was played by Bela Lugosi, returning to his role with Universal for the first time since his first appearance in 1931. In this film, the Count was apparently impervious to sunlight and even cast a reflection. Once more the monsters suffered apparently final deaths, but there was a brief end piece when Abbott and Costello hear a mocking message from the Invisible Man (the voice of Vincent Price).

All in all, the film was good fast slapstick comedy, although it may have offended horror movie fans who liked to take their monsters more seriously. Aside from minor sequences in other films, this comedy concluded the major Universal preoccupation with Dracula.

It was a period marked by a code of good taste. Universal did not attempt to show nauseating special effects of blood spouting from vampires or victims, relying on stimulating the imagination of filmgoers, in the same way that in literature the best ghost stories do not need revolting descriptions and vulgar details. All this was to change, however, in the second main chapter of Dracula and Monster movies.

Now the production scene shifted to England and a long series of Gothic horror movies produced by Hammer Films, under James Carreras. What I have called the 'Sledge-Hammer Films' made a special feature of realistic special effects of spouting blood, agonising close-ups of vampires screaming in agony as they were staked in their coffins, dwelling also on gnashing fangs as vampires sucked blood from their victims. There was also a strong anti-feminist aspect of featuring beautiful young women as either vampires or ravaged victims.

It is difficult to say whether this was a matter of changing taste in audiences, now craving something more terrifying than the tired old clichés of horror films, or whether Hammer Films themselves created a public taste for the sensational and repulsive. Probably it was a mixture of both.

Hammer commissioned scriptwriter Jimmy Sangster to write a new script of Stoker's *Dracula*, released in 1958 as *Dracula* in the United Kingdom, but retitled *Horror of Dracula* in its U.S.A. release by Universal-International, now acting as distributors. In their time, the Universal horror films had suited all tastes. The timid were really scared, while more sophisticated audiences treated horror films as camp entertainment, good for a giggle. It was perhaps to be expected that this latter group should be catered for in the mixing of monsters with comedians like Abbot and Costello.

Hammer changed all that. As one film critic put it - the vampire image was revamped. Now the fangs of actor Christopher Lee were displayed, dripping with blood, vampires screamed in agony as they were staked, blood spouting in fountains, all in full colour. Special effects became ever more realistic. In contrast to the stilted slow-moving Dracula of Bela Lugosi in 1931, Christopher Lee's portrayal was quick, athletic, and animal-like in ferocity, although still retaining the neat black clothing and theatrical cloak.

Dracula (1958) was directed by Terence Fisher, an extremely competent director, who also became responsible for further Hammer films. In this initial Hammer *Dracula*, many liberties were taken with Stoker's story. The film opens in Transylvania where Jonathan Harker has been sent by Van Helsing to investigate stories of local vampirism on the pretext of indexing the Count's library and journals. The part of Renfield is absent from the film. Harker himself becomes a vampire and is impaled with a stake by Van Helsing. Various scenes were eliminated by the British censor as too gruesome, but the film made a lot of money.

This success inspired Hammer to create a sequel titled *Brides of Dracula*, released in 1960. However, this film did not feature Dracula himself, assuming that his disintegration into dust in the preceding film was final, and instead introduced his disciple, the evil Baron Meinster, played by a handsome wavy-haired David Peel.

Although this film did well, it was clear that audiences preferred the original Count Dracula character, so scriptwriters racked their brains to create convincing ways of revivifying him from apparent final disintegration. Eventually they came up with *Dracula, Prince of Darkness* in 1966, with Christopher Lee again resuming the central role. The revival was achieved by gathering the dust of the Count and placing it in a coffin, over which a blood-bespattered corpse is laid. At the end of the film, the Count apparently drowns in the icy waters surrounding his castle - but obviously not for long, for in 1968 Hammer produced *Dracula Has Risen From the Grave*. In one scene, the 'dead but he won't lie down' Dracula was even shown able to wrench a stake from his own heart!

It would be tedious to enumerate all the various Hammer variations on a theme, with titles like *Taste the Blood of Dracula*, *Scars of Dracula*, *Dracula A.D. 1972*, *The Satanic Rites of Dracula*, but Hammer continued to prosper, making a Dracula film every year. The tired old clichés of the power of the crucifix and the efficacy of stakes through the heart were given many plot twists, and always the final demise of the Count, however convincing, left room for a miraculous resurrection in yet another Hammer movie.

What Hammer demonstrated was that on relatively low budgets, with the aid of ingenious scripts and blood-bespattered special effects, it was possible to derive a considerable and continuing revenue from infinite variations on the theme of Count Dracula and vampires. In this series, actors like Christopher Lee and Peter Cushing, with directors like Terence Fisher, played a notable part. Hammer also produced many other horror films, based on stories by Edgar Allan Poe and other writers. Worthy also of mention is their thriller *The Vampire Lovers*, directed by Roy Ward Baker, 1971, which faithfully reproduced much of the erotic Lesbian atmosphere of Sheridan Le Fanu's vampire thriller *Carmilla*, on which it was based.

Meanwhile foreign film makers in Spain, Italy, France, Germany, Japan, Korea, Argentina, the Philippines, and elsewhere produced scores of movies on Dracula and vampire themes. Surely no other fictional character has ever exerted such a world-wide influence!

In the third chapter of Dracula films, the genre of the horror film became increasingly dominated by vulgarity and bad taste. In the U.S.A., many films were bizarre and often sleazy. After *Billy the Kid versus Dracula* came *Kiss Me Quick* (a Russ Meyer nude film), and *Ghost in the Invisible Bikini*. Other uninspiring titles included *Dracula Meets the Outer Space Chicks*, *Mondo Keyhole*, *The Mad Love of a Hot Vampire*, and the first homosexual Dracula film, titled *Does Dracula Really Suck?* Inevitably the under-privileged black filmgoers were treated to *Blacula* (1972) with a climax in a sewage disposal plant, and a sequel *Scream Blacula Scream* (1973).

Andy Warhol, with his flair for high camp sleaze and bad taste, got into the act with *Blood for Dracula*, directed by Paul Morrissey in 1975. This Dracula needs the blood of virgins, becoming increasingly scarce. In the end scenes Dracula's arms and legs are hacked off before impalement.

I find it extraordinarily depressing to wade through the record of scores of increasingly cheap, decadent exploitation movies, squeezing the last drop of blood from a character created by Bram Stoker in

A poster for the French version of *Dracula* (1958) starring Christopher Lee a single novel written in his limited spare time. This flood of basically uninspiring films stimulated new excesses in the horror film genre, in which every artifice of realistic special effects is used to shock and nauseate viewers in order to make a fast buck.

From time to time, there have been genuine attempts to return to Stoker's original novel and tell that story with some integrity. In 1975, Dan Curtis had directed a feature length television film *Bram Stoker's Dracula*, with Jack Palance giving a memorable performance as the Count. Although this omitted some materials from Stoker's novel, it made an honest attempt to keep to the atmosphere and detail of the book in a good script by Richard Matheson, and may have influenced the production of the recent Francis Ford Coppola movie of the same title. Another worthwhile attempt at the original novel was the 1979 *Dracula*, directed by John Badham, with the leading role played by Frank Langella, who had earlier performed the part hundreds of times on the stage.

A much vaunted Spanish/Italian/English/West German co-production *El Conde Dracula (Count Dracula)* in 1970 was to have been directed by Terence Fisher, but in the event was assigned to Jess (Jesus) Franco, who lacked Fisher's style and verve as a director. In spite of good performances by Christopher Lee as the Count and Herbert Lom as Van Helsing, and a reasonably close adherence to Stoker's plot, the film is disappointingly pedestrian, and pathetically tries to develop suspense by the device of overuse of a zoom lens.

Special mention should be made of Werner Herzog's *Nosferatu - Phantom der Nacht* (1979), with memorable performances by Klaus Kinski, Isabelle Adjani, and Bruno Ganz. The film is notable for its pastel shades, and is virtually a loving tribute to F.W. Murnau's original 1922 classic.

More recently, Francis Ford Coppola's movie *Bram Stoker's Dracula* (1992) claimed to follow Stoker's book closely, and did indeed keep to a number of plot situations and circumstantial details, like the use of a typewriter and a phonograph. However, it grafted on to Stoker's story a plot with a prologue about Vlad the Impaler in fifteenth century Wallachia. In James V. Hart's script, Vlad, distracted by the premature death of his beloved princess, dedicates himself to the Devil and is able to manifest himself as a shape-changing Count Dracula, searching for his reincarnated princess through the centuries; she eventually manifests in the shape of Mina in Victorian England. This far-fetched attempt to fuse together two separate stories destroys any value in the detail of Stoker's plot, and indeed, actively neutralises it. The film also has some anachronisms. After an appearance as a somewhat campy Count Dracula, with bouffant hairdo, Dracula suddenly appears in London as a long-haired dandy with modern sun glasses. Moreover he meets Mina at a cinematograph show in 1897 London. The images on Coppola's screen are much more advanced than the crudities of cinema in 1897, and the introduction of what James V. Hart called 'a sly cinematic joke' - projecting images derived from Coppola's prologue of Vlad the Impaler's battles in fifteenth century Transylvania, together with a soft porn nude show - is wildly anachronistic. The Vlad the Impaler secondary plot seems to me a misjudged gimmick, and while one can admire Coppola's technical virtuosity, I believe he was badly served by his scriptwriter, and the film bears less fidelity to the spirit of Stoker's novel than Murnau's pirated *Nosferatu*. It is notable, incidentally, that both Coppola and scriptwriter James V. Hart had seen and greatly admired Murnau's film.

However, the release of Coppola's movie in Dublin in early 1993 revived interest in Stoker and his book. In that sense, Coppola brought Stoker back to Ireland, where Bram had been sadly overlooked since his death in 1912. Newspapers, journals, radio and television shows were devoted to Stoker and Dracula, emphasising that Stoker was an Irishman. Sadly, little was said about his real work in the theatre, in popularising informed theatregoing in Dublin years before the Abbey Theatre, and in devoting himself to management of Henry Irving's career. The same weak jokes of the "Fangs awfully" kind were revived by journalists who should have known better.

Dracula was a remarkable sensational novel, written in Stoker's spare time. It took ancient superstitions and created a new mythology in a thrilling allegory of the age-old problems of good and evil, love and death, but it is marginal to the real character of Stoker and his life work. It tells us nothing of the courage and devotion to duty and art which characterised Stoker's life in the theatre world.

It is just over seventy years since Murnau's silent film *Nosferatu* brought *Dracula* to the movie screen. During that period there has been a sad decline in cultural taste and values, reflected in and often stimulated by films. Just as horror comics vulgarised and degraded literature by crude and tasteless text and images, so modern horror movies have served a sub-culture of realistic and violent sado-masochism that degrades public values and behaviour. As with other populist exploitation, it also finds its intellectual high camp apologists, who carry banners for total freedom in the arts. In modern cinema, through skilful and shocking special effects, limbs are torn off, eyeballs gouged out, heads exploded in torrents of blood, women tortured as well as raped, culminating in under-the-counter snuff movies in which people are actually murdered in front of a movie camera. All this mirrors and stimulates a crime-ridden drug-obsessed society, where pornography, violence and sexual perversion are commonplace, and rather than purge our emotions with pity, terror or laughter, the under-privileged are invited to join the orgy or create their own. Our children, fed on surreptitiously viewed horror and sex films, torture animals, steal fast cars and kill people; their drug gangs lie and steal to maintain the habit, and vandalise decent neighbourhoods by senseless violence.

All this sleazy decadence is a long way from the *Dracula* of Bram Stoker, in which the horrors of ancient evil make a final appearance, to be defeated by the forces of individual courage and decency. Traditionally, the tragedy and farce of the theatre carried a sub-text of the eternal verity of good defeating evil in the Aristotelian dramatic concept of purging by pity, terror or laughter.

It was surely ironic that Stoker's passion for theatre should have been overwhelmed by the newer medium of cinema, which was a relatively trivial and naive novelty at the time he published his novel in 1897. He remained faithful to the theatre as a major art form until his death in 1912. Even then, cinema stories were still rather primitive, and it was not until ten years later in 1922 that Murnau's *Nosferatu* showed that silent cinema could be a powerful and artistic medium. Since then, there have been many great films in both silent and sound cinema, but there has also been an influential stream of decadent movies, augmented by the newer media of television and home video.

I noticed in a video magazine recently an advertisement offering 'rare horror, mondo, gore, sleaze and exploitation films, many unavailable elsewhere'. With unblushing cynicism the advertiser signed himself 'Vomit Bag Video'.

Bram Stoker and the great actor Henry Irving, whom he served so faithfully for more than a quarter of a century, were men of the theatre, dedicated to inspiring dramas and comedies, and would have been astonished and disturbed by a sleazy movie and video industry that has eclipsed their achievements and ideals. For what use are the arts if they cannot inspire us to a greater understanding of life and a determination to play our part in making society a better place to live in?

As Chairman of the Bram Stoker Society, it is my hope that we can spread a public awareness of Stoker's chivalrous character, his many achievements, and his devoted work in theatre, in place of the universal cliché that he was merely the man who wrote *Dracula*.

14. I LIKE PLAYING DRACULA

~ Bella Lugosi (1935)~

I like playing 'horror' parts on the screen. This may surprise you, but let me explain my point of view.

There is a popular idea that portraying a monster of the Dracula type requires no acting ability. People are apt to think that anyone who likes to put on a grotesque make-up can be a fiend. That is wrong.

A monster, to be convincing, must have a character and a brain.

The screen monster produced by mere tricks of make-up and lighting will never thrill an audience. It will make them laugh! It is just a machine which does not understand what it is doing.

Now, imagine this creature with a character, with reasoning power and certain human mental facilities. It is no longer a machine. It can think.

Such a monster is able to thrill an audience. It can plot against the hero and heroine. It is a menace which must be combated by brains, not by running away.

We are all more afraid of cunning than brute force. Therefore, the monster must have cunning to trap his victims—physical strength is not enough to convince an audience.

Now, perhaps, you begin to see why I find the playing of fiends interesting!

When I am given a new role in a horror film, I have a character to create just as much as if I were playing a straight part.

Whether one thinks of films like *Dracula* as 'hokum' or not, does not alter the fact; the horror actor *must* believe in his part. The player who portrays a film monster with his tongue in his cheek is doomed to failure.

An example of this occurred not very long ago. An actor, whose name I

Bella Lugosi & Carol Borland in a publicity still for *Mark of the Vampire*

will not mention, played the part of a sinister foreign villain. He had been used to straight parts, and he went into this film laughing at himself. He did the correct villainous actions, but he had his tongue in his cheek all the time.

The villain was completely unconvincing and as a result the film was a flop at the box office. Later, an almost exactly similar character was played by another actor. He took it seriously. Audiences believed in the villain and the film was a success.

I am not saying that I personally take seriously these vampires and monsters as such. I am saying that ONE must take them seriously when one is portraying them.

In playing Dracula, I have to work myself up into believing that he is real, to ascribe myself the motives and emotions that such a character would feel. For a time I *become* Dracula – not merely an actor playing at being a vampire.

A good actor will 'make' a horror part. He will build up the character until it convinces him and he is carried away by it

There are of course, plenty of tricks of the trade to be employed, such as effective make-up, clever photography, a threatening voice and claw-like gestures with the hands. These are important in the 'hokum' film and must be used. But even they must be employed with intelligence or they will fail to thrill.

To leave the theoretical discussion of so-called monsters, there is another reason why I do not mind being 'typed' in eerie thrillers.

With few exceptions, there are, among actors, only two types that matter at the box office. They are heroes and villains. The men who play these parts are the only ones whose names you will see in electric lights outside the theatre.

Obviously, I cannot play a juvenile part — you will not find me competing with Clark Gable or Robert Montgomery! Therefore, I have gone to the other extreme in search for success and public acclaim.

Every year a number of films with fantastic or supernatural characters are made, and will, it seems, continue to be made, whatever may happen to the horror 'cycle' of pictures. I have deliberately specialised in such characters — and I firmly believe there will be suitable roles for me for a long time to come!

15. NOSING AROUND NOSFERATU

~ Jeanne Keyes Youngson ~

"Nosferatu" is a pirated film version of Bram Stoker's *Dracula*. The book was believed to be still in copyright in 1921 when the film was started, although it was never really protected by Library of Congress registration in the U.S. The title of the film was changed to "Nosferatu" (adapted from a Romanian term meaning 'not dead') and Dracula himself renamed "Count Orlock". The names of other characters were also changed, and the plot set the destination of the death ship as Bremen in Germany, instead of Whitby in England.

None of these changes protected the film from relentless prosecution for infringement of copyright by Stoker's widow, Florence. She forced the director, Murnau, to withdraw the film in July 1925, but in spite of a court order to destroy all negatives, the film was released in 1929. Until recently, the prints which survived were shown only to film societies and other specialised audiences in a shortened version. We now realise that the illegal prints which survived were only the ghost of a masterpiece by the great German director, F.W. Murnau. A recently restored version is some twenty minutes longer than any prints previously shown, and it is possible to appreciate the full beauty of the settings and camerawork, and the masterly way in which Murnau built up the sequences, developing parallel action. It is now easy to understand why the modern German film director, Werner Herzog, was inspired to remake the film with loving care in 1979, in homage to Murnau.

Murnau's film is still regarded as the best screen version of the Dracula story.

Bram Stoker's widow, Florence, sold Stoker's working notes for *Dracula* at auction in 1913 and received approximately two pounds, or about ten dollars, for them. The following year she published *Dracula's Guest*, a collection of short pieces, including a chapter from *Dracula* which had been deleted because the book was thought to be too long.

Florence was, at this point, living in reduced circumstances. When Bram was in the employ of Henry Irving, the Stoker home on Cheyne Walk was elegantly furnished and their circle of friends was, to quote Miss Jean Brody, *la creme de la creme* of society.

Now, on William Street in Knightsbridge, Florence had to depend on the small amounts that dribbled in from *Dracula* the novel, and on handouts from her son, Noel, who was working as an accountant. Since their relationship had always been rather strained, she did not expect, nor did she receive, much financial assistance from him.

Once, during an interview, Vincent Price told about going to Florence Stoker's mews house for tea and recalled that her precious memorabilia included portraits by Rossetti, Burne-Jones, and her old flame, Oscar Wilde. She also had presentation copies of books by the greatest authors of the day, and, Price added with a sigh, she was still very beautiful. As it also turned out, she was also a tiger when sinking her teeth into the problem which surfaced when she heard that a German film company had, without permission, used her husband's story in a movie entitled *Nosferatu*.

In 1922 she joined the British Incorporated Society of Authors, presumably to recruit their support in what was to become a major and most unpleasant and tiresome conflict.

While the German entrepreneurs had never heard of Florence Stoker, they were obviously familiar with *Dracula*. Albin Grau, a designer, painter and architect, had picked up on the potential of a vampire theme as film material and made numerous sketches evoking the mystical, magic effects the movie was intended to express.

Much to my surprise, while researching this essay at the Franklin College Library in Lugano, Switzerland, I learned of a story Albin Grau related, regarding the *Dracula* dispute. While it may or may not be factual, it is an interesting sidelight which causes one to wonder why more was not made of it at the time.

Grau claimed that in 1916, when he was in the army in Serbia, he met an elderly peasant who told a story about his father who had died in the early 1880s and had been buried without receiving the proper sacraments. The old man had then started haunting the village in the form of a vampire. The peasant subsequently produced an official document which stated that a man called Morowitch had indeed been exhumed at Progatza in 1884, showing no signs of decomposition and with an impressive set of long sharp teeth.

The Lord's Prayer was said over the exhumed body, which was then staked. The vampire, known in Serbia as a "Nosferatu", gave a loud groan and expired.

Years later, said Grau, while travelling through the Tatra Mountains, he met one of his old army chums who had witnessed the entire affair and who confirmed Grau's memories, including having also seen the official document. It is certainly within the realms of possibility that Albin Grau provided the title and the idea of *Nosferatu*, using the overall framework of Bram Stoker's novel.

The horror films coming out of Germany during the 1920s were a reaction to the humiliations and defeats the country had been experiencing for years, especially during and immediately after the First World War.. *The Cabinet of Caligari*, *The Golem*, *Waxworks*, *Warning Shadows* and *The Hands of Orlock* expressed and reflected the desire for escapism, with *Nosferatu* yet another example of these intentionally disturbing expressionistic horror movies.

Once the idea of a vampire film had taken hold, Grau and his partner, Enrico Dieckmann, hired one Friedrich Wilhelm Murnau to direct *Nosferatu*. Murnau had, in the past, worked with the famous Max Reinhardt, and was, as one sees in the movie, deeply influenced by Reinhardt's use of light and shadow, which resulted in unique, ethereal, and often frightening, effects.

Murnau was tall, nearly six feet five inches, had red hair, and was extremely handsome. He exuded an air of authority, and, according to Janet Gaynor, with whom he later worked in Hollywood, frequently and deliberately terrorised the actors working under him, especially those from Germany. He wore, she claimed, a blue jump-suit and a piece of blue glass around his neck, which - in her mind - took the place of a monocle and conveyed a sense of incomparable elegance.

Born on 28 December 1888, in Bielefeld, Germany, Friedrich Wilhelm Murnau was an imaginative child and an insatiable reader. His early dreams of producing plays were realised when his brother built a large toy theatre with a revolving stage, theatrical lighting, and even a trap door. On Sundays, the children produced plays, charging small fees to family and friends who attended the performances.

Wilhelm did indeed grow extremely tall, which was one of the reasons he later preferred directing to being an actor. He had, in fact, studied Philology in Berlin, then transferred to Heidelberg to study art history and literature. It was during this period, while performing in a student play, that he was seen by Max Reinhardt who took him on as a member of his travelling theatre school. Murnau's stage career was interrupted when he went into the army as a pilot during the First World War. His father later wrote:

> "One day he got lost in a thick fog and landed in Switzerland and was interned at Andermatt. A competition was then being organised in Switzerland for the best production of *Marignano*, a popular national drama. Every canton could compete and so could the internees. My son won first prize and was acclaimed when the play was performed in Bern."

These accolades were a turnabout for his father who had never been pleased about Wilhelm's theatrical aspirations.

For a while, Murnau completely dropped his family, former friends and schoolmates. He did not see or contact them, nor did he answer any of their letters. The only person he wrote to was his mother, and, very rarely, his brother. He later did spend a Christmas with his brother and wife, presumably before leaving for the United States of America.

Nosferatu, the movie, was eventually finished. Florence Stoker heard about it and went to work with a vengeance. Members of the British Incorporated Society of Authors which she had joined correctly surmised that the only reason she had become a member was to enlist their support with the *Nosferatu* problem. G. Herbert Thring was the secretary of the society and, as such, had to take the brunt of Florence's incessant nagging. He and the society eventually put the matter into the hands of their Germany attorney, a Dr. Wronker-Flatow, who lived and worked in Berlin.

Oh, my! Florence Stoker was mad. Florence Stoker was persistent. Florence Stoker wanted justice. Above all, Florence Stoker wanted money.

In August of 1922, G. Herbert Thring contacted Florence and told her that the society was doing all it could, but . . .! Reading between the lines, Florence knew that the society really didn't give a damn. Undaunted, she still had some irons in the fire, and immediately took advantage of certain influential friends who had ties within the society. On 22 August, 1922, a Power of Attorney was sent to Dr. Wronker-Flatow in Berlin. At this point, Florence discovered that the movie was actually being shown in Budapest, which - if this were possible - further incensed her. She had been told that the film company had declared bankruptcy, and yet they were now collecting money from the movie, money that was rightfully hers. Was there no end to their insolence?

The situation dragged on and on. The society and poor G. Herbert became more and more exasperated. And still no conclusions were reached. Florence Stoker was trying to obliterate what was already being considered a classic movie and a lot of people were involved. As we have already seen, Florence Stoker was a determined woman. And why not? By now the copyrighted *Dracula* was virtually her only means of support.

Eventually, on 20 July, 1925, word came from Berlin assuring the beleaguered society and a jubilant Florence Stoker that all prints and negatives of *Nosferatu* were to be destroyed. Florence breathed a sigh of relief, but - alas! - all too soon. Almost immediately, she heard that a British Film Society was being formed and one of the movies on its schedule was none other than . . . *Dracula*! by F.W. Murnau. Now, on top of everything else, they were claiming authorship. The weary British Incorporated Society of Authors advised her to send a registered letter forbidding any showing of the film anywhere, any time, any place, by any one! More letters and phone calls followed, advising the film society that the movie was "stolen goods". And then, incredibly, there was more. The movie was being offered to theatres throughout England - and no one was able to locate those responsible for this development. Was reality imitating art?

The cinematic vampire had flapped over country and channel and could obviously turn up whenever it wished. The vampire had achieved a life of its own and could move throughout the world at will.

Which ultimately brings us to the movie itself, the very film that caused Florence Stoker, and a lot of others, so much pain and anxiety.

Count Orlock, or sometimes Orlof, was a tall, thin, bald creature with pointed ears and arched eyebrows. He had lived for centuries in a castle in Transylvania, and, in 1838, decided to set sail for Bremen in search of fresh blood. Doesn't this sound familiar! After leaving a trail of destruction and death, he falls madly in love with his real estate agent's wife, Ellen Hutter. Aware of his horrendous and evil reputation, Ellen sacrifices herself to keep him up and awake until dawn. The fact that he never blinks and becomes even more grotesque as the movie progresses adds to the film's general macabre horror. I cannot resist mentioning David Skal's[1] humorous comment on how different the film would have been, had Max Schreck at some point appeared wearing a black wig, garter belt and net stockings with holes. No, Murnau would never have been that crass. As we all know, the Transylvanian terror was terminated by the rays of the sun while wearing a dark sort of uniform that emphasised his ashen face and elongated talons.

Did I say terminated? Well, it was the end of Florence's battle, more or less. But definitely not the end of *Nosferatu*. At about this time, something absolutely astounding came to light regarding the movie. It was discovered that, due to a loophole in the copyright law, *Dracula* had always been in the public domain in the United States of America, and, to top it off, Bram Stoker himself was to blame for not having deposited two copies of his work with the American Copyright Office. In other words, anyone in the U.S.A. could have produced any adaptation of *Dracula* they wished. But, of course, no one had known this back in 1922 when Mrs. Stoker started lowering the boom. Florence died in May of 1937. She left over £6,000 in cash (about $30,000) and bequests to the Victoria and Albert and London Museums, and books to the London Library. One of her gifts to the London Museum was a pastel portrait of Henry Irving which Bram Stoker had purchased from Irving's estate. Incredible as it may seem, but true to form, Henry Irving left poor old Bram absolutely nothing in his will.

In 1979, Werner Herzog directed *Nosferatu the Vampyre*, which, according to Jean Marigny, author of *Vampires, the World of the Undead*, was

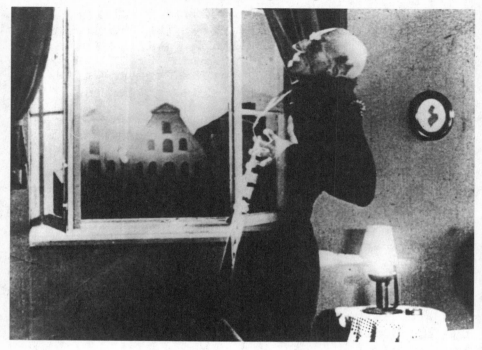

a return to the source. Klaus Kinski re-used Max Schreck's make-up, but did not manage to convey the abject horror that Schreck brought to the role.

Herzog referred to his film as being an homage to Murnau, but a number of critics thought the film self-consciously "arty". Some may not, of course, agree with these critics, but as one wag recently remarked, there are a lot more showings of Murnau's *Nosferatu* than of Herzog's these days.

Nosferatu continues to turn up in various media forms throughout the world. Thank goodness Florence isn't here to see it.

1. Skal (David J.): *Hollywood Gothic -*
The Tangled Web of Dracula
from Novel to Stage (W.W.Norton, 1990)

16. INTERVIEWS WITH PETER CUSHING AND CHRISTOPHER LEE

~ John Exshaw ~

AN INTERVIEW WITH PETER CUSHING   *12th May 1993*

Exshaw: In your first volume of autobiography, you mentioned your fondness for the films of Tom Mix. What other memories do you have of the silent era?

Cushing: Lillian Gish I was rather mad about, I thought she was smashing. They were wonderful, those pictures by D.W. Griffith. And, as a very young chap, I saw a serial called 'The Nibelungs' and I was so impressed - I must have been only about five or six - and there was a chap having a bath in dragon's blood. Nothing on - shot on his back, of course - and as he was bathing in this blood, a leaf fell down and settled on him. That part of him, wherever it was, didn't get covered by the magic blood so that was his Achilles' heel. And that impressed me enormously. I thought that was super. Of course, there was no dialogue but they had the music. They played Wagner and that started my great love of his music.

Exshaw: Despite (or perhaps because of) the commercial success of the Hammer films, director Terence Fisher has received scant attention from the critics. Can you tell us something about his personality and working methods?

Cushing: Where he was so good was - he was an editor, and I think every film director could be well helped by being an editor; you waste not and want not. He knew exactly what he wanted, and for Hammer it was manna from heaven because they pared things so much down you began to see the white meat, you know. Because they made things very economically, but very well. And that was what Hollywood could not understand or believe. They could not believe that *[The Curse of] Frankenstein* was made for £65,000. They just would not believe it. But where Hammer was so clever, they'd get someone like Terence Fisher whom they knew would pare it exactly down so there was no fussing around. He knew exactly where he was going to cut, where he was going to put it together.

[He was] a very quiet little chap, very inarticulate and always open to suggestions because he said "actors are invariably right about some things. They can be wrong, but I am not very good at telling them things. But I like them to do it. And I say now this is wonderful and then I am able to elaborate upon it. If I don't like it, I say no, but I always explain why." So he was that type of director. Everyone adored working with him. Very calm and, as I've said, absolutely sure of himself. Never threw his weight about and always brought the pictures back in on time. Or under schedule sometimes. When we first did 'Frankenstein', Jimmy Carreras [head of Hammer Films] said, "You'll get it done in two weeks, won't you?" And he [Fisher] said, "Uh, no. They must have three weeks, actually." "What!!" said Jimmy, "you'll ruin me before we start." And, of course, when, after about its first week, it had already paid for itself four times over, Jimmy Carreras couldn't believe it.

Exshaw: Your grandfather, Henry Cushing, was a member of Irving's Lyceum Theatre. He would presumably have known Bram Stoker very well?

Cushing: Yes, yes, indeed. But my dear Dad, bless his heart, seemed to be reticent about that for some extraordinary reason. I mean, no family could be more stage-bound than his was. As you say, his father was with the Laurence Olivier of his time for twenty years. . . . But I think it was because in those days all actors were still regarded as 'rogues and vagabonds', and Dad was a bit worried that I was going that way.

Exshaw: Did you ever feel, as Christopher Lee did, that the later Hammer 'Dracula' films were not doing justice to Stoker's creation?

Cushing: From Christopher's point of view, I agree entirely because as he said, "now I'm just in a corner, curling my lips and hissing." You see, trouble is, dear boy, when you do a film like, say, 'Frankenstein', you have to have - not a mad scientist, but a chap like the anatomist, Knox, who's trying to do something for the future, for man's good. So he makes what turns out to be a monster. Well, you are stuck with that. If you are going to make 'Frankenstein', you've got to have that element. The same with 'Dracula' - you must have a chap who comes and sucks ladies' jugulars. So it's awfully difficult for the poor old scriptwriters to get variations on that same theme. . . .

But Van Helsing could take little variations, and it was always a very interesting part to play. . . . It was a goodie against a baddie, and people liked me in the part. I was quite wrong for it inasmuch as when it was first mooted I said lovely, but, dear old boy - I said to Sir James Carreras - I said this fellow is an old man who speaks double-Dutch. Well, why don't we get an old man who speaks double-Dutch? Because - I was told - there isn't an old double-Dutch man who people want to go and see. They want to go and see you. And as they like you as you look now - why, I don't know, ha, ha, ha - you are playing as you look, like this. So I said alright. . . .

But it still comes back, the original one is still only the best one to do. I haven't seen the one with Tony Hopkins as Van Helsing - I saw a clip of him which I thought was wonderful. And he played it with an accent, which was absolutely right. But to me, dear old Christopher is the definitive Dracula. I think he's absolutely super in it because he's got this extraordinary majestic thing about him. Of course, he is very aristocratic - his family are Italian aristocrats - which is wonderful for the part.

Exshaw: What do you recall about working with Christopher Lee, Vincent Price, and John Carradine on *House of the Long*

Shadows?

Cushing: That was wonderful. The four of us, at last they got us together. . . . When you think of the diversity of those four people : Christopher; Vincent, who is the biggest rogue in the business. I mean, such a lovely rogue, but he's got a wonderful wit, you know; John Carradine; and myself. I mean, you couldn't think of four more disparate characters but we were all playing brothers in the thing. . . . I would put him [Carradine] down as a Southern gentleman, [but] you see, you didn't have much time to fraternise because the whole thing was shot in a house in the country so you couldn't really speak louder than that because of the sound. It was work all the time, hardly ever ceased. Also, I'm never much of a chatter when I'm playing a part. I have to think about it and not be distracted. And we all had separate rooms to dress in and relax . . .

Exshaw: In the past, you've made an important distinction between 'terror' films and 'horror' films. Could you elaborate on that?

Cushing: Yes, I did make that point and I often do, and so do the fans, you know. Because horror to me is something that really - what is happening now in the world is horror. In Ireland, in Bosnia and all this. That is real horror. And what happens in road accidents, that's horror. Do people really want to see that sort of thing? I don't think so. But mystery and fantasy, yes, I think it uses the imagination, it takes them away from that, and that is what all the fans - and not from my generation but this generation - write. . . . They say we love those films because they leave such a lot to the imagination. Good always prevails over evil. That was a wonder, that, to me, for this day and age. It's a wonderful thing to hear. And you do not rely heavily upon special effects, and they call today's horror films 'chainsaw' [films]. I can't bear 'em! . . . Who on earth do they think they're catering for when they make these wretched films? I suppose they do make them for the American market. I don't know. . . .

CHRISTOPHER LEE ON DRACULA   *1st May 1993*
- interviewed by John Exshaw

Exshaw: I've read that you always carried a copy of Stoker's book on the set when you were playing Dracula. Is that true?

Lee: I think that's got a bit out of hand. What happened was that I always said that I had read the book and within the limitations of the script on the first one *Dracula* (1958) - they disintegrated over the years - I tried to present Stoker's character as he described him in the book. Now that was not done correctly physically, or visually either. And I might have brought the book down on occasions desperately trying to get some of Stoker's lines out in the scene which, over the years, I think I managed to do about three or four times. They were pretty short ones too. Because this was to me, as an actor playing the part, the great disappointment - that for some extraordinary reason, having written a good script, they chose to ignore Stoker's lines and dialogue almost totally.

As far as my character was concerned, there was some Stoker in the first one, and not in the second (*Dracula - Prince of Darkness*, 1965), because I refused to speak the lines of the script which is why there was no dialogue. I said, I'm not saying these lines, and they didn't have time to rewrite them. And then progressively over the next three or four, whatever there were I did for them, there was less and less meaning to it. And I kept on saying, well look, here's the book, look at these great lines, look at these great things. Can't we slip them in somewhere? No. They never agreed and that is why they became progressively less and less interesting and that is why I was determined to stop them.

A fact that isn't generally known, and I can say it now because Jimmy Carreras (Sir James Carreras, head of Hammer films) is dead, is that I turned down the last four films. I said, I don't want to do them because this isn't Stoker's character, these aren't Stoker's stories. If you must do one, let's do 'Dracula's Guest' which has never been done. . . . And so I used to get these calls at home from Jimmy saying to me, I beg you, I beg you. You must do these films. And I said, why? He said, because, a)

I've already sold them, and, b) think of the people you will put out of work if you don't do them. Think of your colleagues who will not get a job as a result and think of the technicians.

It is a pretty terrible thing to say to an actor. It is indeed monstrous. As a result of that I used to give way, but it certainly wasn't my wish to do so.

Exshaw: But surely by the early Seventies, you had enough clout to force Hammer to listen?

Lee: No, they wouldn't listen. They wouldn't listen because my agent knew that I wouldn't do it myself. I didn't consider that I should be bothered by having to explain all this myself. That's what an agent is for. He refused to do it. He was too frightened that he would have a quarrel with Hammer and they wouldn't use his other clients. I used to try with the producers, people like Tony Hinds and Michael Carreras and Tony Nelson-Keys. Sometimes they would go along but the thing was cast in concrete by that time. So if I added to it then the scene was longer which gave problems to the director, it gave problems to the editor, and so it was terribly difficult for me. Sure, I had enough clout, but it didn't result in anything.

Exshaw: What do you recall of the film *Count Dracula*? (*El Conde Dracula*, made in Spain in 1970 by Jess Franco).

Lee: That was a marvellous opportunity, totally wasted. It's the only time that Dracula has been presented on the screen physically exactly as described by Stoker. A tall, thin old man with a long white moustache, totally dressed in black, who gets younger and younger during the film. It's the only time that's been done. The only time. And also I brought some of Stoker's lines in. I actually made a bit of that speech about the great battle he describes four hundred years before, which of course was his, against the Bulgars and the Turks - "but now the wind sighs through the broken battlements of my home", and so on and so forth. I actually got those lines out, believe it or not. I just insisted.

However, Herbert Lom as Van Helsing and Klaus Kinski as Renfield - not a bad start. What was wrong with it is that it was shot so cheaply and on such a tight budget that, I mean, it was starting with a long shot, medium shot and then close-up, all on a zoom! Consequently it's close-up to close-up, there's no reverse. Do you realise that I played scenes with Herbert Lom but he wasn't even there? He played scenes with me and I wasn't there. So, if you're going to make a picture that way . . . well, you can't save it.

Exshaw: What is your opinion of Coppola's *Bram Stoker's Dracula*?

Lee: I can't make any comment on that because I saw that in Paris at the premiere and I actually introduced Coppola to the French audience from the stage. And Francis Ford Coppola is a great film-maker, no question whatsoever - a great film-maker, and he's done some wonderful things. I actually read the script long before they made the film and it was, in terms of the sexual element, pretty strong, to put it mildly. I think a lot was cut. The film looked marvellous. It was a great achievement to make it all in the studio, on stage. But it's not Bram Stoker's story. Part of it is. It's the first time he's been properly killed. But even then he wasn't killed, if you see what I mean. And it wasn't Stoker's story and it wasn't Stoker's characters as he described them. That's all I'm prepared to say. For obvious reasons I can't make any further comment. If I said I thought it was the greatest film I've ever seen, that it was absolutely brilliant and wonderful and marvellous and staggering, people would say, "well, of course he says that. He wants to make a film with Coppola." If I said I think it's the worst film I've ever seen, that it was awful, it was grotesque and it was a travesty, people would say, "well, of course he says that because he wasn't in it."

17. THE SIGN OF THE CROSS

the story of an ancient symbol

~ Leslie Shepard ~

We are all familiar with those horror films in which the evil vampire is repulsed and defeated by the hero brandishing a crucifix, or making the sign of the cross with a sword hilt or even two sticks. In spite of dazzling special effects, the convention is now somewhat ridiculous, and it is not surprising that one or two films have (may I say) revamped the cliché by portraying a vampire which is impervious to such trivial prophylactic. If there was any efficacy in the sign of the cross in modern times, I am sure that schoolteachers would use it to control an unruly class, or perhaps even policemen might wave it in front of desperate criminals.

But the belief in the magical power of the cross is a very ancient one, and it is still a critical element in exorcism rituals to assist in driving out evil spirits.

It is generally assumed that the occult power of the cross is of Christian origin, since the cross is the key symbol of the crucifixion of Jesus, and still plays a large part in the rituals of Christian churches, where it symbolises redemption and eternal life. However, the powerful symbol of the cross is of greater antiquity, and, like many pagan beliefs, was adopted by the Christian religion as late as the fourth or fifth century AD, reinforcing the association with the crucifixion. Crucifixes with the image of Christ appeared around the seventh or eighth century, and the cult of the cross became most popular in the thirteenth century.

But thousands of years before the Christian era, various forms of the cross were engraved on pagan temple walls and sarcophagi. The cross was widely revered by the ancient Incas, tattooed on the foreheads of Patagonians, used in the rites of Druids. In Africa, Hottentot women kept wooden crosses above them during confinement. The Maoris of New

Zealand wore crosses as amulets. Crosses were found on the sacred stones of North and South America, Mexico, and Central America, as well as on the enigmatic giant statues of Easter Island. Thousands of years ago, the *Rig-Veda*, a sacred Indian scripture, symbolised the fire god Agni by two crossed sticks, representing the fire drill.

It has been calculated that there are some three hundred variant forms of the cross symbol. Of these, the major forms are the two crossed lines, the *T* shape or Tau, the Tau with a loop at the top, the swastika, the cross combined with a circle, and the Maltese Cross (resembling four triangles joined at the apex). In turn, each of these forms has many variants, with different associations.

The simple Greek Cross with four equal length arms is a symbol of the four elements and the four seasons. Different mythologies have used this cross to symbolise the four rivers of Paradise. In Buddhism, there is the four limbed Damba tree or tree of life, with four sacred streams (north, south, east and west) flowing from its cross. The Dakota Indians of North America used this cross to represent four winds issuing from caverns in which the souls of men were stored before incarnation. The Greek cross dates back to prehistoric times, and has been found engraved on pebbles circa 10,000 BC at Le Mas d'Azil, a cave in the French Pyrenees. In arithmetic this cross symbolises addition, and thus, perhaps the growth of families.

The equal cross on its side is generally known as St. Andrew's Cross or Saltire, symbolising perfection. In ninth century Scotland, this cross is said to have appeared in the sky to Achaius, King of the Scots, and Hungus, King of the Picts, before their battle with Athelstane, King of England. After their victory, Achaius and Hungus walked barefoot to the Kirk of St. Andrew, and vowed to accept his cross as a national emblem. This cross is also named décusés, meaning the number ten. The Roman sign for ten is a cross made of two *V*'s or fives. The ancient Chinese used this sign in the form of two crossed fire sticks. This cross survived as the mark of an illiterate individual unable to write a signature, and is also the arithmetical sign for multiplication.

If the perpendicular stem of the cross is longer than the horizontal, this is generally called a Latin cross or *crux immissa*. Although this is the form favoured by the Christian crucifix, the actual crucifixion is believed to have been the Tau or T-shaped cross, used in executing criminals. After scourging, the criminal was forced to carry the cross to the place of execution, then laid naked on the cross and nailed to it as it lay on the ground, sometimes after it was erected. Crucifixion in this manner was a common Roman punishment for criminals, dissidents, and slaves, and widely employed. Alexander Jannaeus, who reigned 104-78 BC, is said to have crucified eight hundred Jews of Jerusalem in one night, slaying their wives before their eyes. The punishment of the cross was common among the Scythians, the Greeks, the Carthaginians, and the Germans, as well as the Romans. When Alexander the Great conquered the city of Tyre in 332 BC, he crucified two thousand of the inhabitants.

Incidentally, crucifixion was not necessarily intended to cause death. It is recorded in the Gospels that when Christ and the two thieves had been crucified for six hours, the soldiers came to kill them and found the thieves were still alive. Pilate 'marvelled' to hear that Christ was already dead. The fact that he was speared by a soldier was reported only in the fourth Gospel 'that ye might believe', presumably for those who doubted that Christ died (*John* 19:34-35). If nailed to a cross for several hours, such a victim might even survive if carefully removed to a cold tomb.

Crucifixion itself appears to have been a modification of the older punishment of impaling, used around two thousand years BC. It was not the invention of the tyrant Vlad Dracula in fifteenth century Transylvania. In 702 BC, Sennacherib said of the rebel Ekron chiefs: "I impaled them on stakes." Assyrian pictures show victims suspended on upright stakes pierced through their breasts.

The Tau cross is named after the Greek letter *T*. It was widely revered in the pre-Christian era. In Scandinavian mythology it was the double hammer of Thor, and thus a symbol of lightning, rain, and fertility. As late as the nineteenth century, German peasants would use the sign of the cross to banish thunderstorms, not because it was a Christian symbol, but because it represented the hammer of the God Thor. The Tau was considered a divine symbol by the Mexicans, who named it the Tree of Life and Tree of Our Flesh, and consecrated it to the god of rain. Candidates for the mystery religion of Mithras, a rival of Christianity, received the mark of the Tau on their foreheads; the rites included a eucharistic ceremony. In Egyptian symbolism, four Taus were sometimes placed back to back to form a large cross, indicating the flaming sword that guarded Paradise in all the four quarters of the universe.

The most common variant of the Tau in ancient Egypt was the Ankh or crux ansata, a Tau with a loop at the top, used as a symbol of divinity. It was associated with the major deities and featured in many inscriptions. Maat, the goddess of truth, was often depicted presenting the Ankh to the sun, source of life, indicating that life and truth are eternal. The Ankh was also widely shown in the hand of a god or king, sometimes held to the nostrils. It was generally regarded as the supreme symbol of life, power, immortality, and generation, the key to the life-giving rise and fall of the river Nile.

The Maltese Cross is formed by four triangles with their apexes meeting in the middle, and features in heraldry and in knighthood orders. The Moki Indians of North America used it as a symbol of virginity. It was the badge of the Knights Templars, founded in the twelfth century to recover the Holy Land, although their secret rituals honoured the pagan god Baphomet, and involved spitting on the Christian cross.

Latin crosses are often combined with a circle, often used as a symbol of the sun. The Latin cross with a circle in the centre featured widely in Celtic crosses, probably dating from the tenth century, and distributed throughout Ireland and Scotland.

One of the most ancient forms of the cross is the swastika, also known as fylfot (an old Anglo-Saxon term meaning "many footed"). This is an equal armed cross with a short line projecting from each arm. These four projections may all point right or left, indicating positive and negative aspects of divinity. Swastikas have been found inscribed on prehistoric clay figures of animals. In Central and South America, the swastika was a symbol of the rain god. It has been widely used in various contexts. It has been found in early North America as well as the Greek fortress of Mycenae, among the Etruscans in Italy, and on third century sword hilts in Denmark. The major origin was in ancient India, and the name 'swastika' itself is Sanskrit for "So be it", with a connotation of auspiciousness, good fortune, and the mystical significance of life itself. The author Rudyard Kipling noted that the swastika was used in India as a protection against fire and water or thieves, that Hindu traders opened their account books with the sign of the swastika as an auspicious beginning of the year.

There is considerable literature on the swastika symbol and its diffusion and meanings. It was used by Hindus, Jains, Buddhists, and also by the peoples of ancient China, Japan and many other countries. In recent history, it has an evil connotation in its desecrated use by the Nazi Party in Germany. Some time between 1870 and 1912, perhaps as an offshoot of the translation of ancient Indian religious texts by Professor Max Müller and others, it was seized upon by fanatical cultists who used it as a Nordic or Germanic symbol, popularising the term 'Aryan' as applied to race. Prominent amongst these cultists was Lanz von Liebenfels, who founded the Order of New Templars, using as his symbol a swastika with both left and right pointing arms, i.e., a cross of four T-shaped arms joined at the centre. Guido von List, an associate of von Liebenfels, founded his own cult of the Armanen, and used the conventional swastika symbol. In 1909, at the age of twenty, Hitler took over the pro-Aryan and anti-Semitic racial theories of these fanatics, used them in his book *Mein Kampf*, and adopted the swastika as the symbol of his Nazi Party, where it became a powerful focus of evil. After stealing the ideas and insignia of these cultists, Hitler banned von Liebenfels and his movement on coming to power.

In all its various positive forms, the cross was a pre-eminent symbol of divinity, a key of life, truth, redemption, the power of nature and procreation long before Christianity. Even the Christian rosary originated in ancient India.

Yet in spite of the powerful significance of the Crucifixion, the cross was not immediately adopted by the early Christians as the supreme symbol of their faith, perhaps because of the shame attached to the ancient punishment of criminals. In the Old Testament, *Deuteronomy* 21: 22-23, it is stated: "He that is hanged is accursed of God", referring to criminals hung on trees as gibbets. Later the Apostle Paul wrote in *Galatians* 3:13: "Christ hath redeemed us from the curse of the law, being made a curse for us; for it is written 'Cursed is everyone that hangeth on a tree'".

There is archetypal significance in the ancient pagan concept of redemption from sin through the sacrifice of a god or a substitute for the divine, perhaps originating in animal sacrifice and ancient eucharistic ceremonies. Among various crucified figures are Thammuz of Babylonia (3,200 BC), Iao of Nepal (622 BC), Hesus of the Celtic Druids (834 BC), Quetzalcoatl of Mexico (587 BC), Mithras of Persia (600 BC or earlier). Other divine figures which were sacrificially slain included Krishna of India, Horus and Osiris of Egypt, Prometheus of Greece.

It is clear that as late as 211 AD, Christians neither desired or adopted the cross as a sacred symbol, because pagans not only adored crosses, but a cross with a man on it. Tertullian, an early Christian father of the second and third centuries, wrote to the pagans scornfully: "The origin of your gods is derived from figures moulded on a cross. All those rows of images on your standards are the appendages of crosses; those hangings on your standards and banners are the robes of çrosses." When denying the charge of idolatry made against Christianity, the Christian Father Minuncius Felix stated in 211 AD: "As for the adoration of the cross which you object against us, I must tell you that we neither adore crosses nor desire them. You it is, ye pagans, who worship wooden gods; who are the most likely people to adore wooden crosses, as part of the same substance with your deities. . . . Your victorious trophies not only represent a cross, but a cross with a man upon it."

In the early period, the symbol of Christ was a lamb, and it was not until after 600 AD that the sixth synod of Constantinople (Canon 82) ordained that instead of the lamb, the figure of a man fastened to a cross should be the Christian symbol; this was confirmed by Pope Adrian I. For a time, a simple cross was placed next to the lamb, then the lamb put on the cross, much as the ancient Israelites had prepared the paschal lamb on two spits, horizontal and vertical, centuries before.

With the rise of Christianity as a new but initially proscribed sect, the cross had been a secret mark traced with a finger on the forehead, much as today Freemasons have secret signs. The Old Testament had recorded that the prophet Ezekiel had a vision in which a mark on the forehead of the righteous "that sigh and cry for all the abominations" would denote those who would be spared when the city was destroyed and the people slaughtered. (*Ezekiel* 9:4). This mark was believed to be the *T*-shaped cross, the final letter of the Hebrew alphabet, which came to signify the last days when the world would be destroyed and reborn.

Down the centuries, the belief in the magical power of the cross was enhanced by legends of miracles associated with it. The most famous account was the *Legenda Aures Sanctorum*, a medieval romance compiled by Jacobus de Voragine, Archbishop of Genoa. This was first printed in English by William Caxton, Britain's first printer, at his press in Westminster, London, in 1483. It became a best-seller immediately. In the same year, an edition printed at Kuilenberg, Netherlands, by Jan Valdener, contained sixty-four wood engravings which appear to have been reproduced from an even earlier block book. Similar illustrations of this legend were widely featured in churches in Troyes, France, frescoed along the walls of the choir of St. Croce of Florence by Agnolo Gaddi. Pietro della Francesca also illustrated the legend in frescoes in the chapel of the Bacci in the Church of St. Francesco at Arezzo.

The legend tells how Helena, the mother of emperor Constantine, discovered the remains of the true cross after a celestial vision. In her seventy-ninth year she was said to have travelled to Jerusalem where she located the site of the crucifixion and found the three crosses concealed under a statue of Venus, so that the Christians who might wish to adore Christ should appear to address homage to the goddess. The true cross was distinguished from the crosses of the two thieves by its miraculous power to cure sickness. In the quaint phraseology of the time, this discovery was known as "The Invention of the Cross", an early meaning of the word.

The Golden Legend is too lengthy to give more than a brief outline here, but it begins with the Tree of Life in Paradise, where a cherub gave three seeds from the tree to Seth, son of Adam, to be placed in his father's mouth at the time of death. Three trees grew from the burial, linking into one. Under this tree, David bewailed his sins. Solomon cut the tree down to make room for his palace, but it sprang up again and defeated the masonry until Solomon cast it away, where it was found by the Queen of Sheba. It was buried and the pool of Bethesda dug over it, which had miraculous properties to heal the sick. When the time of crucifixion drew near, the wood of the tree rose to the surface, where it was found by the Roman executioners seeking a beam for the cross. Significantly, the cross illustrated in the legend is the Tau shape. When Jerusalem was plundered, the true cross was carried away by the king of Persia, but recovered by Heraclius on September 11th, 615 AD, a day afterwards celebrated as the Feast of the Exaltation of the Cross.

Pagan and Christian legends have merged over the centuries in the archetypal story of the Tree of Life in the Garden of Paradise, the punishment of banishment through sin, the promise of expiation through divine sacrifice. In the Teutonic North, tree worship was common, since the tree was sacred to Odin, who hung there nine days and nights wounded, as a sacrifice. That tree was Yggdrasil, the world tree, whose roots are in hell and whose branches spread to heaven.

Belief in the magical power of the cross persisted amongst isolated peasant communities in Eastern Europe, and especially Transylvania, and, surprisingly, quite recently among the Pennsylvania Dutch people of America. The term "Dutch" is a corruption of "Deutsch", since these were German-speaking settlers, later intermarrying with French, Irish and Scots, but retaining a distinctive folklore which included a belief in Hexerai or witchcraft. In 1819, John George Hohman published a popular book of hex or spells and charms which is still reprinted today and still believed in by the credulous. This was *The Long Lost Friend*, or *Pow-Wows*, containing arts and remedies for man and beast. Typical spells include "A Good Way to Stop Bleeding", "A Sure Way of Catching Fish", "How to Cause Thieves to Stand Still". Such spells all involved making the sign of the cross, and the book itself contains the great spell : "Whoever carries this book with him, is safe from all his enemies, visible or invisible; and whoever has this book with him cannot die without the holy corpse of Jesus Christ, nor drown in any water, nor burn up in any fire, nor can any unjust sentence be passed upon him, so help me." This is sealed by a large Latin cross flanked by two smaller crosses.

The games and chants of children often contain many remnants of ancient beliefs. The term "faynights" or "Fains" used by schoolchildren to demand a truce during fights is a survival of medieval English "fain I" meaning "I decline", in turn derived from the Old French "se feindre", meaning to excuse or back out, especially in battle. This truce is consolidated by making a rudimentary cross by entwining the first two fingers of the right hand. The crossed fingers indicate an authoritative banishment, like brandishing a crucifix, although I suspect it has little effect on modern playground bullies. However, even today grown-ups still talk of keeping their fingers crossed in order to ensure success or avert misfortune.

Why should a symbol have been believed to exert miraculous power? Firstly, because it was accompanied by persuasive reports of miracles; secondly, because the requirement for actual miracles appears to be absolute faith and willpower. For thousands of years, Hindus have made *yantras* - magical diagrams inscribed on precious metals, or even in sand, where the correct shape is said to accumulate power, together with the *mantras* or religious sounds which accompany the *yantras*, just as churches and other sacred buildings in the West are believed to concentrate powerful spiritual vibrations in their architecture. The movements of priests and congregations in rituals, and the apparatus associated with them - the altar, vessels, bread, wine, and cross - are held to accumulate divine power in a kind of spiritual geometry. But as belief in the divine declines, so do miracles cease to be reported, life becomes secularised, and religion a kind of folklore. In a materialistic modern world, where vampires are portrayed in horror films for sensationalist emotional entertainment or just a sophisticated giggle, it is little wonder that brandishing a crucifix should have no real power over vampires or the evils of the modern world.

A brief word here regarding garlic or "stinkweed" as it has often been called, since it was also used in connection with the cross to repel demons, witches and vampires, as well as alienate one's friends and lovers. Garlic was regarded as something of a cure-all, antiseptic and prophylactic against many diseases, including plague, in addition to its virtue in adding culinary savour. Aristotle cited it as a spring tonic and also a cure for hydrophobia. Bullfighters in Bolivia used to carry a clove of garlic into the ring to prevent the bull from charging. The historian Flavius Josephus recorded that workers building the Great Pyramid received rations of garlic and onions to give them energy; garlic was also regarded as an aphrodisiac. In India, renunciates who sought spiritual enlightenment through the rigorous practice of yoga were forbidden to eat garlic or onions in their simple diet.

Garlic has a special connection with the cross, since it was associated with the dread Greek goddess Hecate, Queen of the Dead. Her statue was erected at cross-roads, where the intersection created a vast endless cross in the ground. Garlic was carried by travellers, and often placed at the cross-road to propitiate the goddess.

What are we to make of the fact that the Cross was a supremely sacred sign many centuries before the crucifixion of Jesus Christ? Earlier religions undoubtedly revered the ritual sacrifice of a divine saviour on a tree or cross, linked with the change of the seasons, the death of winter, the rebirth of a new spring, and the resurrection of the soul.

Some authorities have suggested that such archetypal symbols are so basic to human experience that history itself becomes shaped into legend. Others have argued that the archetypal symbols of pagan religions prefigure the Christian story. At all events, there is a universal symbolism at the roots of human experience that is inextricably entangled in the dreams, myths and histories of religions, a poetry of the soul that gives meaning and direction to human progress through life.

In 1866, the Reverend Sabine Baring-Gould, a remarkable scholarly and versatile Anglican vicar, archaeologist, folklorist, historian, novelist, author of the well loved hymn *Onward Christian Soldiers*, published an essay on the pre-Christian origins of the cross, in which he concluded :

"For my own part, I see no difficulty in believing that it [the cross] formed a portion of the primeval religion, traces of which exist over the whole world, among every people; that trust in the Cross was a part of the ancient faith which taught man to believe in a Trinity, in a War in Heaven, a Paradise from which man fell, a Flood, and a Babel; a faith which was deeply impressed with a conviction that a Virgin should conceive and bear a son, that the Dragon's head should be bruised, and that through shedding of blood should come remission. The use of the cross, as a symbol of life and regeneration through water, is as widely spread over the world as the belief in the ark of Noah. Maybe, the shadow of the Cross was cast further back into the night of ages, and fell on a wider range of country, than we are aware of . . . It is more than a coincidence that Osiris by the cross should give life eternal to the Spirits of the Just, that with the cross Thor should smite the head of the Great Serpent, and bring to life those who were slain; that beneath the cross Muyses mothers [in South America] should lay their babes, trusting by that sign to secure them from the power of evil spirits."

18. Bram Stoker in Irish – Dracula's Guest

Bram Stoker's novel has been translated into many different languages. It was only natural that there should also be an Irish language version, and this was published in 1933 by Oifig Díolta Foillseacháin Rialtais, Dublin. This translation by Seán Ó Cuirrín has been long out of print and is an eagerly sought rare book on the secondhand market.

In celebration of the Centenary of first publication of *Dracula*, a completely new Irish translation has now been produced by An Gúm, and this will be warmly welcomed by lovers of the Irish language.

In our own Centenary publication, we can also add an interesting additional Irish language contribution.

Stoker's notes and research materials for his novel, now preserved in the Rosenbach Foundation Library in Philadelphia, indicate various changes in the development of his story, notably two sections which were eventually not used in the published work. The first one dealt largely with a correspondence regarding Count Dracula's intended purchase of an estate in England and Jonathan Harker's involvement. However, it slowed up the story and was no great loss. The second section, probably omitted for reasons of length, is a vivid account of part of Jonathan Harker's journey to Transylvania, during the course of which he is attacked by a werewolf. In 1914, two years after Stoker's death, this chapter was published by his widow, Florence, in a book titled *Dracula's Guest and Other Weird Stories*. It has special interest, since it contains a detail of the discovery of the grave of the Countess Dollingen of Gratz in Styria, indicating Stoker's indebtedness to J. Sheridan Le Fanu's earlier vampire novel *Carmilla*, first published 1871. Carmilla was a vampire countess of Styria (an Austrian province). Stoker had at one time planned to set his own story in Styria.

Dracula's Guest is a fascinating prologue to Stoker's story, and to celebrate the new Irish translation of *Dracula* we are now presenting, for the first time, an Irish language translation of this missing chapter.

AOI DRACULA

arna aistriú go Gaeilge ag Alan Titley

Bhí an ghrian ag soilsiú go lonrach ar Munich, agus bhí an t-aer lán d'aoibhneas luath an tsamhraidh nuair a thosaíomar ar ár n-aistear. Tháinig Herr Delbrück (maître d'hotel an Quatre Saisons, ina raibh mé ag fanacht) anuas go dtí an carráiste go díreach agus sinn ar tí imeachta. Bhí a cheann nocht aige, ghuigh sé dea-thuras orainn, agus fad is a bhí a lámh i gcónaí aige ar mhurlán an charráiste, dúirt sé le fear an chóiste:

'Cuimhnigh nach foláir duit bheith ar ais anseo roimh thitim na hoíche. Tá cuma na gile ar an spéir, ach fós tá bagairt sa ghaoth aduaidh a thuarann stoirm gan choinne. Ach tá a fhios agam nach mbeidh sibh déanach,' agus rinne sé miongháire anseo agus dúirt 'mar tá a fhios agaibh cén oíche atá againn anocht.'

D'fhreagair Johann 'Ja, mein Herr,' go daingean, chuir a lámh lena hata agus d'imigh leis go gasta. Nuair a bhí an baile fágtha inár ndiaidh againn rinne mé comhartha leis stopadh agus d'fhiafraigh mé de:

'Inis dom, a Johann, cén oíche atá anocht againn?'

Rinne sé comhartha na croise agus d'fhreagair ar nós cuma liom: 'Walpurgis nacht.' Agus leis sin thóg sé amach a uaireadóir, ceann mór airgid seanfhaiseanta Gearmánach chomh mór le meacan. Bhailigh sé a chuid malaí le chéile agus chroith a chuid guaillí amhail is dá mbeadh mífhoighne éigin air.

Bhí fhios agam gurbh é seo an tslí a bhí aige le cur in aghaidh na moille seo nach raibh aon ghá leis, déarfá, agus luíos siar sa charráiste ag tabhairt an noid dó dul chun bealaigh. Ghluais sé leis go gasta faoi mar a bheadh sé ag iarraidh an bhris ama a thabhairt isteach. Ba dhóigh leat insa tslí dúinn gur chaith na capaill a gcloigne san aer le neart amhrais ó am go chéile. Níor fhéad mé gan féachaint thart orm agus iarracht den eagla ag dul tríom anois is arís. Lom go maith a bhí an bóthar, mar bhíomar ag gluaiseacht linn trí mar a bheadh ardán gaofar ann. De réir mar a bhíomar ag dul ar aghaidh chonaic mé bóthar thíos uaim a raibh an chuma air gur ghabh sé go fiarlóideach trí ghleann caol nach raibh siúl mórán daoine air. Chuir an gleann sin cluain orm sa tslí dom gur iarr mé ar Johann stop, agus ba chuma liom dá mbeadh sé i bhfeirg liom dá bharr. Nuair a stop sé dúirt leis go mba mhaith liom dul an bóthar sin síos. Chrom sé ar leithscéalta a dhéanamh go tiubh, agus rinne comhartha na croise go minic fad is a bhí sé ag caint. Phrioc seo an fhiosracht ionam agus dhírigh mé ar cheisteanna breise a chur air. Ba sheachantach a chuid freagraí, agus d'fhéach sé go síoraí ar a uaireadóir mar olc orm. Ar deireadh dúirt:

'Féach, a Johann, is mian liom dul síos an bóthar sin. Nílim ag iarraidh ort teacht muran áil leat é; ach inis dom cén fáth nach mian leat teacht liom, sin a bhfuilim ag iarraidh.' Ba dhóigh leat gurbh amhlaidh gur chaith sé é féin anuas den bhosca mar fhreagra orm, a ghasta is a shroich sé an talamh. Ansin dhírigh sé a lámha amach agus é ag impí go tréan orm gan dul. Bhí dóthain Bhéarla ar éigean trína chuid Gearmáinise ionas gur thuig mé éirim na cainte uaidh. Shíl mé go raibh sé ar thob rud éigin a rá liom fad na haimsire, rud éigin a chuir an croí trasna air ní foláir; ach is amhlaidh gur chuir sé srian leis féin gach uair agus deireadh 'Walpurgis-Nacht!' fad is a bhíodh sé ag déanamh comhartha na croise.

Rinne mé iarracht dul chun áitimh leis, ach ba dheacair é nuair nár thuigeas a theanga i gceart. Bhí sochar an chúrsa leis, gan amhras, mar in ainneoin gur thosaigh sé ar Bhéarla briste garbh a labhairt, d'iontaíodh sé ar a theanga dhúchais nuair a d'éiríodh sé corraithe, agus d'fhéachadh ar a uaireadóir gach uair dá ndéanadh. Is ansin a d'éiríodh na capaill suaite agus dhéanadh siad bolú ar an aer. Leis seo, d'iompaigh an lí air, d'fhéach timpeall agus sceimhle air, thug léim chun tosaigh, chuir na capaill ar sréin, agus threoraigh ar aghaidh fiche éigin slat iad. Rinne mise é a leanúint agus d'fhiafraigh mé de cén fáth a ndearna sé seo. Rinne sé comhartha na croise mar fhreagra orm, dhírigh a mhéar ar an áit a d'fhágamar inár ndiaidh, tharraing an carráiste i dtreo an bhóthair eile agus dúirt, i nGearmáinis i dtosach, agus ansin i mBéarla:

'É curtha - eisean iad féin a mharaigh.'

Ba chuimhin liom sean-nós faoina n-adhlactaí daoine a chuir as dóibh féin ag an gcrosbhóthar. 'Sea, tá a fhios agam. Duine a chuir lámh ina bhás féin. Sea, más ea!' Ach ní fhéadfainn a thuiscint ó thalamh an domhain cén fáth a raibh sceimhle ar na capaill.

Fad is a bhíomar ag caint chuala fuaim mar a bheadh idir geoin agus amhastraigh. Bhí sé i bhfad uainn; ach d'éirigh na capaill corraithe arís, agus b'é dícheall Johann iad a shuaimhniú. Bhí sé mílítheach, agus dúirt:

'Dealraíonn sé gur mac tíre atá ann - ach fós féin níl aon mhac tírí timpeall na háite seo.'

'Nach bhfuil?' arsa mise, á cheistiú; 'nach fada ó bhí na mac tírí i gcóngar na cathrach?'

'Ó, is fada, fada,' ar seisean, 'san earrach agus sa samhradh; ach ní fada a bhí siad anseo leis an sneachta.'

Fad is a bhí sé ag déanamh peataireachta ar na capaill agus á suaimhniú, ghluais scamaill dhorcha go gasta trasna na spéire os ár gcionn. Shéalaigh an gealán, agus d'imigh briota fuar gaoithe tharainn ós íseal. Ar éigean gur phuth féin a bhí ann, agus nuair a tháinig an ghrian amach arís ba dhóigh leat gur mhó de shamhail ná de rud ar bith a tharla a bhí ann. D'amharc Johann amach as faoi bhun a láimhe ar íor na spéire agus dúirt:

'An stoirm sneachta, tagann sé arís roimh am ró-fhada.'

Ansin d'fhéach sé ar a uaireadóir arís, agus lomdíreach fad is a bhí greim daingean aige ar an srian - mar is amhlaidh go raibh na capaill fós ag cartadh lena gcosa agus ag croitheadh a gcinn - léim sé in airde ar a bhosca faoi mar a bheadh an t-am buailte umainn leanúint den turas.

Tháinig stuaic bheag orm agus níor chuaigh mé caol díreach isteach sa charráiste.

'Inis dom,' arsa mise, 'faoin áit seo a ngabhann an bóthar ann,' agus dhírigh mé mo mhéar an bealach síos.

Rinne sé comhartha na croise arís eile, dúirt paidir faoina anáil, agus d'fhreagair: 'Tá sé neamh-bheannaithe.'

'Cad tá neamh-bheannaithe?' d'fhiafraigh mise.

'An sráidbhaile.'

'Mar sin tá sráidbhaile ann?'

'Ó, níl, níl in aon chor. Ní chónaíonn aon duine ann na céadta bliain.'

Rinne seo mé a phriocadh: 'Ach dúirt tú go raibh sráidbhaile ann?'

'Bhí.'

'Cá bhfuil sé anois?'

Leis sin bhrúcht scéal fada amach as agus bhí an Ghearmáinis agus an Béarla chomh mór trína chéile ann gurbh ar éigean a thuig mé i gceart cad a bhí á rá aige. Ach go hachomair thuig mé uaidh go bhfuair fir bás ansin na céadta bliain ó shin agus gur cuireadh ina gcuid uaigheanna iad; agus gur chualathas fuaimeanna faoi chré na cille, agus nuair a hosclaíodh na huaigheanna go bhfuarthas fir agus mná a raibh rua na beatha iontu, agus a raibh a mbéal dearg le fuil. Agus mar sin, d'fhonn a mbeatha féin a shlánú (is ea, agus a n-anamnacha freisin! - agus rinne sé comhartha na croise anseo arís) is amhlaidh gur theich a raibh fágtha go baill eile, áit ina raibh cónaí ar na beo, agus ina raibh na mairbh marbh, agus nach raibh siad - nach raibh siad rud éigin eile. Ba léir go raibh eagla air na focail dheireanacha seo a rá. De réir mar a ghabh sé ar aghaidh leis an eachtra is ea is mó a d'éirigh sé corraithe. Ba dhóigh leat go raibh a chuid samhlaíochta gafa lastuas de agus go raibh sé i lár spairne na sceimhle - bhí a aghaidh traochta, é ag cur allais, agus ar crith agus ag féachaint ina thimpeall, amhail is go raibh uafás éigin lena nochtadh féin ar an machaire méith faoi sholas na gréine. Ar deireadh, le teann cráiteachta, d'éigh sé:

'Walpurgis nacht!' agus chomharthaigh dom an carráiste le dul isteach ann. Thosaigh a raibh d'fhuil Shasanach ionam ag coipeadh leis seo. Sheas mé i leataoibh beagán agus dúirt:

'Tá eagla ort, a Johann, tá eagla ort. Imigh leat abhaile; fillfidh mé im aonar; déanfaidh an choisíocht mo leas.' Bhí doras an charráiste ar oscailt. Thóg mé mo mhaide siúil dara den suíochán - bíonn sé i gcónaí liom ar mo chuid saoire - agus dhún mé an doras. Dhíríos mo mhéar siar ar Munich agus dúirt leis: 'Imigh leat abhaile, a Johann - ní haon chás don Sasanach é Walpurgis-nacht.'

Ba chorraithe ná riamh anois iad na capaill, agus bhí Johann ag iarraidh srian a choimeád leo, agus ag an am céanna ag impí orm gan aon ní baoth a dhéanamh. Bhí trua agam don chréatúr bocht a lomdháiríre is a bhí sé; ach mar sin féin níor fhéadas gan gáire a dhéanamh. Bhí a chuid Béarla imithe glan uaidh um an dtaca seo. Rinne sé dearmad leis an sníomh aigne a bhí air gurbh é an t-aon tslí amháin a bhí aige le dul i bhfeidhm orm ná mo theanga féin a labhairt, agus mar sin lean sé leis ag geabstaireacht liom sa Ghearmáinis a bhí aige ó dhúchas. D'éirigh mé dóthanach de. Nuair a bhagair mé abhaile air chas mé d'fhonn an bóthar isteach sa ghleann a thabhairt orm féin.

D'iontaigh Johann a chuid capall i dtreo Munich le comhartha uaidh go raibh deireadh dóchais sroichte aige. Chuir mé mo chuid meáchana ar mo mhaide agus d'fhéach ina dhiaidh. Ghluais sé leis fan an bhóthair ar feadh tamaill: ansin ar mhul cnoic tamall uaim nocht fear caol ard. D'fhéadfainn oiread sin a fheiscint go soiléir i bhfad uaim. Nuair a tháinig sé i gcóngar na gcapall chrom siad ar bheith ag léim is ag ardú a gcos, agus ansin ag seitrigh le halltacht. Níor fhéad Johann srian a choimeád leo; d'imigh siad de ráig bhuile an bóthar síos. D'fhair mé iad go dtí gur chuaigh siad as amharc, ansin lorgaigh mé an stróinséir, ach ba léir, leis, go raibh sé siúd imithe.

Bhí éadroime ar mo chroí nuair a chuaigh mé síos an fobhóthar i dtreo an ghleanna a raibh col ag Johann leis agus a bhí ag dul i ndoimhne uaim fad an achair. Ní raibh cúis dá laghad, dar liom, leis an gcol sin uaidh; agus ní foláir nó gur choisigh mé liom ar feadh roinnt uaireanta an chloig gan puinn machnaimh a dhéanamh ar an am den lá ná ar fhad na mílte, agus is deimhnitheach nach bhfaca mé duine ná teach ar mo shiúlta. Dar leat gur fásach ó bhun barr siar amach a bhí san áit. Ní fhéadfainn a rá gur thugas é seo faoi deara go speisialta go dtí gur tháinig mé ar imeall scaipthe coille ar chasadh an bhóthair dom; is ansin a tuigeadh dom go raibh lomsceirdiúlacht fholamh na háite ar ghabhas tríd tar éis dul i bhfeidhm orm.

Shuigh mé síos chun mo scíth a ligean, agus chrom mé ar fhéachaint ar an tír máguaird. Taibhsíodh dom go raibh sé pas beag níos fuaire ná mar a bhí nuair a thosaigh mé - ba dhóigh liom go raibh geonaíl bhog éigin i mo thimpeall, agus uair um á seach, i bhfad lastuas díom, mar a bheadh béicíl mhúchta éigin. Agus nuair a d'fhéachas in airde thugas faoi deara go raibh scamaill mhóra mhothallacha ag gluaiseacht leo aduaidh i bhfad thuas. Bhí comharthaí na stoirme a bhí chugainn le léamh ar an tsraith b'uachtaraí den aer. Bhraith mé féin ribe ar an oíche, agus ós rud é gur cheapas go rabhas dulta fuar im shuí dom tar éis m'aistir, thosaíos ar mo chuid siúil arís.

B'é an pictiúr é an taobh tíre trína raibh mé anois ag taisteal. Ní hé go raibh aon ní sonrach ann a luifeá do shúil air, ach bhí aoibhneas áilleachta éigin ag baint leis an iomlán. Níor chuir an t-am aon mhairg orm, agus níor chuimhnigh mé ar conas a shroichfinn an baile arís go dtí go raibh doircheacht chontráth na hoíche ag teannadh isteach orm. Bhí gile an lae téaltaithe ar fad faoi seo. B'fhuaire fós an t-aer, agus ba shoiléire fós gluaiseacht na scamall go hard os ár gcionn. I bpáirt leo bhí mar a bheadh fuaim ina samhlófaí tonntracha ag ruathrúch cois trá agus glam rúnda i bhfad i gcéin mar a bheadh ó mhac tíre, mar a mheas an tiománaí. Mhoilligh mé ar feadh meandair. Dúirt mé liom féin gur gairid go bhfeicfinn an baile tréigthe, agus mar sin lean mé orm, go dtí gur tháinig mé ar ball go dtí cluain leathan talún a raibh cnoic á ia isteach mórthimpeall. Bhí crainn ar mhaoilinn na gcnoc chomh fada síos leis an machaire, agus iad breactha, leis, ina ngarráin thall is abhus ar log is ar léibheann. Lean mé casadh an bhóthair lem shúile cinn go dtí gur chuaigh sé as radharc laistiar den gharrán ba dhlúithe díobh.

Nuair a bhí mé ag amharc uaim tháinig creathán fuachta ar an aer, agus thosaigh an sneachta ag titim. Chuimhnigh mé ar na mílte míle slí de thalamh sceirde ar ghabhas tríd, agus bhrostaigh mé liom ag lorg fothana sa choill a bhí ar mo bhéala amach. Is i ndoircheacht fós a d'fhás an spéir, agus is i dtroime agus i ngastacht a thit an sneachta go dtí go raibh an tír máguaird in aon bhrat geal sneachta amháin ionas go raibh íor na spéire múchta le doiléire aontachta uainn. Ba gharbh an bealach faoi mo chosa, agus níor léir a chuid imeall dom ach go háirithe san áit a mbíodh plaincéidí an bhóthair, dar liom; agus ar ball ní folair nó chuaigh mé ar seachrán ón tslí, mar bhraith mé uaim clúid chrua na cré, agus ba dhomhaine fós a chuaigh mo chosa sa bhféar agus sa chaonach. D'éirigh neart breise sa ghaoith go dtí gur lag liom rith ina coinne. Tháinig fuarnimh ar an aer, agus in ainneoin mo chuid siúlóide thosaigh sé ag goilliúint orm. Is amhlaidh go raibh an sneachta ag titim chomh tiubh sin anuas orm, agus ag gabháil ina chaisí im thimpeall gurbh ar éigean gur éirigh liom mo shúile a choinneáil ar oscailt. Réabadh an spéir lasnairde le splancracha tintrí anois is arís, agus sna léasacha d'fheicfinn uaim dlús mór crann, iubhair agus cíoprais don chuid is mó agus iad ar fad arna gclúdach le sneachta.

Ba ghairid go rabhas faoi fhothain na gcrann, agus ansiúd, sa chiúnas coiteann, d'fhéadfainn seordán na gaoithe os mo chionn a chloisint. Níorbh fhada gur slogadh doircheacht na stoirme i nduibhe na hoíche. De réir a chéile bhí an stoirm ag imeacht léi; mhair sí greas eile i bputhanna agus i séideáin fraochta. Um an am sin ba dhóigh liom go raibh fuaim fhiata an mhic tíre ina mhacalla trí fhuaimeanna eile im thimpeall.

Uair um á seach thagadh ga fánach gealaí trí dhoircheacht thiubh na scamall a chaitheadh solas ar an taobh tíre agus a léireodh dom go rabhas ar imeall dlús crann iubhar agus cíopras. Ós rud é go raibh an sneachta stoptha, shiúil mé liom ón bhfothain agus chrom mé ar an ngnó a iniúchadh níos grinne. Tuigeadh dom go bhféadfainn dídean éigin a fháil i measc a raibh d'fhothraigh fágtha agus ar ghabhas tríothu bíodh siad ar lár nó ná bíodh. Dé réir mar a ghabhas timpeall na roschoille tuigeadh dom go raibh balla íseal ina thimpeall agus nuair a leanas liom fuair mé oscailt ann. Ba chuma nó scabhat iad na crainn chíoprais agus iad ar an mbealach go dtí bloc d'fhoirgnimh éigin. Fuair mé silleadh súl air seo, ar éigean, ach ansin dhubhaigh na scamaill an ghealach agus ghluais mé liom ar an gcosán san doircheacht. Ní foláir nó gur chuaigh an ghaoth i bhfuaire, mar mhothaigh mé creathán ag dul tríom; ach ní raibh dídean ar bith faoi mo chomhair, agus rinne mé glámáil liom ar aghaidh gan treoir.

Stop mé, mar bhí ciúnas gan choinne im thimpeall. Bhí an stoirm imithe; agus ráineodh gur stop mo chroí de bheith ag bualadh i mbá le ciúnas an dúlra. Ach ba ghairid a mhair an ciúnas; mar i dtobainne bhris solas na gealaí trí na scamaill agus tuigeadh thar amhras dom gur i reilig a bhíos. Tuigeadh, leis, dom gur tuamba ollmhór marmair ba ea an cruth cearnógach os mo chomhair, agus go raibh sé chomh geal leis an sneachta a bhí air agus ina thimpeall. Le solas na gealaí tháinig gíoscán garbh na stoirme, ar dhóigh leat air gur ag tosú arís a bhí sí le geonaíl fhada íseal mar a bheadh ag madraí nó ag faolchoin. Bhí alltacht agus uafás orm, agus bhraith mé an fuacht ag dul in ainseal orm go dtí gur shamhlaíos go raibh greim aige ar mo chroí. Agus ansin de réir mar a thit caise sholas na gealaí ar an tuamba marmair bhreisigh ar neart na stoirme, amhail is dá mbeadh sí ag dul siar ar a cúrsa. Ghabh iontas éigin mé, agus chuaigh mé i gcóngar an tuamba féachaint cad a bhí ann agus cad a bhí á dhéanamh ag a leithéid in áit mar sin. Shiúil mé thart air agus léigh mé sa Ghearmáinis os cionn an dorais Dhoraich -

> Cúntaois Dholaingen Gratz
>
> in Stiria
>
> A loirg is a fuair an bás
>
> 1801.

Bhí spíce mhór láidir iarrainn ar bharr an tuamba thuas agus é dingthe tríd an marmar, mar is amhlaidh go raibh an tógáil ar fad comhdhéanta de chlocha ollmhóra daingne. Nuair a ghabhas siar air chonac i litreacha greanta Rúiseacha:

'Is gasta mar a ghluaiseann na mairbh'.

Bhí rud éigin chomh haisteach is chomh neamhchoitianta sa ghnó ar fad gur bhain sé siar asam agus gur chuir sé lagar éigin orm. Don chéad uair riamh tháinig iarracht de chathú orm nár ghlac mé le comhairle Johann. Agus is ansin a buaileadh isteach i m'aigne gan choinne gan iarraidh gurbh í seo Walpurgis nacht!

Walpurgis nacht, nuair a cheaptaí go raibh an diabhal amuigh, agus gur osclaíodh uaigheanna na marbh le siúl inár measc, dar lena lán. Nuair a bhí gach uile rancás ag a raibh de dhrochsprideanna an aeir agus na talún. An áit seo féin ar sheachain an tiománaí é go sonrach. Baile bán na gcéadta bliain ó shin. B'í seo an áit ar cuireadh an duine a chuir lámh ina bhás féin; agus b'í seo an áit ina rabhas gan taca im aonar ar crith leis an bhfuacht faoi bhrat sneachta agus an stoirm bhuile ag tórmach orm! B'é dícheall mo chuid fealsúnachta agus mo chuid creidimh agus mo chuid misnigh gan titim ar lár in aon spairn scéine amháin.

Agus anois bhris séideán bruithne anuas orm. Chrith an talamh amhail is dá mba réab na mílte capall trasna ar a chraiceann; agus an uair seo bheir an stoirm léi clocha flithshneachta ar a sciatháin reoite a raibh oiread nirt iontu go mba dhóigh leat gur ó chranntabhaill Bhailéaracha a tháinig - clocha flichshneachta a leag idir dhuilleog agus chraobh agus a rinne oiread spreas de na crainn chíoprais is go mba dhóigh leat gur coirce scéin iad a gcuid gas. Theich mé liom go dtí an crann ba ghoire dhom; ach ba ghairid gurbh éigean dom a fhágáil, agus an t-aon bhall amháin a thabharfadh dídean ceart dom a lorg, doras domhain Dorach an tuamba mharmair. Chrom mé ansin in aghaidh an dorais mhóir chré-umha, agus fuair mé cosaint éigin ó bhuillí na gclocha sneachta. Ní raibh ann anois ach gur bhuail siad im choinne nuair a léim siad aníos ón talamh agus amach ó thaobh an mharmair.

Chuir mé mo chuid meáchana leis an doras, agus bhog sé uaim á oscailt isteach. B'fháilteach an tuamba féin i séideán cradhscalach mar é, agus bhí mé ar tí dul isteach ann nuair a dhein solas na tintrí corrán os mo chionn a ghealaigh an spéir ó thaobh taobh. Chonaic mé ar an toirt, dar Dia is dar mo bheatha féin, nuair a d'iompaigh mo shúile i dtreo doircheacht an tuamba, bean álainn a raibh lánleicne agus beola dearga aici. Bhí sí, shamhlaigh mé, ina luí romham ar an gcróchar. Nuair a réab an toirneach lasnairde beireadh greim daingean orm agus caitheadh amach san stoirm mé mar a bheadh fathach dom dhíbirt. Tharla gach ní chomh tobann sin go raibh na clocha sneachta ag gabháil stealladh orm sular thuigeas an geit coirp agus anama a baineadh asam. Ag an am céanna leathnaigh mothú láidir diamhair tríom a thug le fios dom nach rabhas im aonar. D'fhéach mé i dtreo an tuamba. Ar an bpointe boise, tháinig splanc tintrí eile anuas ón spéir agus chuaigh caol díreach tríd an staic iarrainn a bhí in airde ar an tuamba. Síos isteach sa talamh a chuaigh sé in aon laom lasrach amháin agus dhein smionagar den mharmar ar an tslí. D'éirigh an bhean mharbh aníos ar feadh meandair pianpháise, an tine mar fháinne ina timpeall, ach múchadh a scread scéine le neart thorann na toirní. B'é manglam seo na nglórtha uafáis an rud deireanach a chuala mé nó gur gabhadh arís ag an ngreim fathaigh mé, agus na clocha sneachta ag stealladh anuas orm, agus macallaí ghlamairt na bhfaolchon san aer máguaird. Agus b'é an chuimhne dheireanach a bhí agam ná cruth doiléir bán ag gluaiseacht faoi mo dhéin amhail is gur chuir na huaigheanna uile a gcuid amhailteanna amach agus go raibh siad ag teacht ina léinte báis tríd an bhflichshneachta chun mé a bhascadh.

~ ~ ~ ~ ~ ~ ~ ~ ~ ~ ~ ~

De réir a chéile chorraigh mo mheabhair arís, dá mba ar éigean é; agus ansin tháinig tuirse an tsaoil anuas orm. Níor chuimhin liom tada ar feadh tamaill; ach ansin thosaigh mo chéadfaí ag filleadh orm. Bhí pianta ar fud mo chos, ach níor fhéadas iad a bhogadh. Bhí mar a bheadh barrliobar orthu. Bhí fuacht nimhneach ar chúl mo mhuiníl agus siar fan chnámh mo dhroma, agus bhí mo chluasa, leis, ar nós mo chos, gan mhothú; fós féin bhí siad ciaptha, ach bhí mar a bheadh teas i lár mo chléibh a chuir aoibhneas orm mar mhalairt. Ba dhóigh liom gur tromluí oíche a bhí ann - tromluí fíordháiríre, más ceadmhach dom a leithéid a rá, mar tuigeadh dom go raibh meáchan trom ag brú ar mo bhrollach ag tachtadh m'anála asam.

Ní foláir nó mhair an tréimhse seo inar chuma liom faoi rud ar bith fada go leor. Ach de réir mar a shíothlaigh sé ní foláir gur tháinig mo chodladh orm nó gur thit mé i bhfanntais. Agus ansin sórt déistin, mar a bheadh tinneas farraige ina tús, agus mian bhuile mé féin a fhuascailt ó rud éigin - n'fheadar cad é. Thuirling ciúnas mór anuas orm mar a bheadh an saol go léir ina chodladh nó b'fhéidir marbh - agus gan fuaim le cloisint ach saothar anála ainmhí éigin i ngar dom. Bhraith mé cimilt the ar mo scornach, agus ansin tuiscint ghléineach ar alltacht na fírinne a chuir an fuacht trí mo chroí agus mo chuid fola ina caise trí m'inchinn. Ainmhí mór éigin bhí ina luí orm agus é ag líorac mo scornaí. B'eagal liom bogadh oiread na fríde, críonnacht éigin ó dhúchas a thug orm fanacht socair ní foláir. Ach tuigeadh don bhrúid go raibh athrú éigin dulta orm, agus d'ardaigh sé a cheann. Chonaic mé súile lasánta ollmhóra an mhic tíre os mo chionn trí m'fhabhraí leathdhúnta. Bhí a chuid fiacla géara geala ag glioscarnaigh ina bhéal dearg leata, agus mhothaigh mé a anáil fhíochmhar shearbh go bláth ar m'aghaidh.

Ar feadh aga eile níor chuimhin liom a thuilleadh. Ansin tháinig drannaíl íseal isteach i mo mheabhair, agus lean sceamhaíl é a chuala arís is arís eile. I bhfad i gcéin, dar liom, d'airigh mé sórt 'Hóla! Hóla!' á ghlaoch ar chuma scata guthanna ag éamh le chéile. D'ardaigh mé mo cheann go faichilleach agus d'fhéach sa treo arbh as a bhí an fhuaim ag teacht; ach bhí an reilig sa tslí orm. Bhí gach re glam fós ón mac tíre ina bhealach aisteach féin, agus chonaic mé solas dearg ag gluaiseacht thart i ngarrán na gcrann cíoprais mar a bheadh an fhuaim á leanúint acu. De réir mar a dhruid na guthanna i ngar dúinn, chuaigh glamanna an mhic tíre i neart agus i ngastacht. Níor leoigh mé corraí ná fuaim ar bith a dhéanamh. Tháinig an solas dearg níos gaire fós dom agus é ag gluaiseacht thar an léirchur bán a shín uaim i ngach treo san doircheacht. Agus ansin i dtobainne tháinig trúip marcach ar sodar amach as na crainn agus toirsí á n-iompar acu. D'éirigh an mac tíre ó mo bhrollach agus thug na cosa leis faoi dhéin na reilige. Chonaic mé duine de na marcaigh (saighdiúirí adéarfainn ar a gcaipíní agus ar a gclócaí fada míleata) ag ardú a raidhfil agus ag déanamh amais. Ghriog compánach dá chuid a lámh in airde agus chuala an t-urchar ina sheordán os cionn mo chloiginn. Is amhlaidh gur cheap sé gurbh é cnap mo choirpsa an mac tíre, de dhealramh. Chonaic duine eile fós díobh an t-ainmhí agus é ag éalú leis, agus caitheadh urchar leis. Agus ansin ghluais an trúip chun tosaigh ar chosa in airde - cuid acu chugamsa agus cuid eile ar thóir an mhic tíre agus é ag dul as radharc i measc na gceann cíoprais faoina gclúid sneachta.

De réir mar a dhruid siad im chóngar thugas iarracht ar éirí ach chuaigh díom, bíodh gur chuala is go bhfaca gach a raibh ar siúl im thimpeall. Léim beirt nó triúr de na saighdiúirí dá gcapaill agus chuaigh ar a nglúine im aice. D'ardaigh duine acu mo cheann, agus chuir a lámh ar mo chroí.

'Dea-scéala, a chomrádaithe!' d'éigh sé, 'Tá a chroí fós ag bualadh.'

Cuireadh slogóg bhranda ansin siar im bhráid; chuir sé feacadh ionam, agus bhíos ábalta ar mo shúile a oscailt agus féachaint im thimpeall. Bhí idir shoilse agus scáileanna ag gluaiseacht i measc na gcrann, agus chuala fir ag glaoch ar a chéile. Theanntaigh siad go dlúth agus lig ualla scéin astu; phreab na soilse de réir mar a tháinig na fir amach as an reilig i mbéal a gcinn mar a bheadh siad gafa ag ainsprid éigin. Nuair a tháinig an chuid a bhí chun tosaigh i ngar dúinn, thosaigh a raibh timpeall orm ag raideadh ceisteanna leo le díocas:

'An bhfuil sé fachta agat, mar sin?

Tháinig an freagra go borb agus go gasta:

'Níl, níl in aon chor! Tar anseo ar an toirt! Ní áit moille í an áit seo, anocht thar oícheanta an tsaoil!'

'Cad a bhí ann?' Cuireadh an cheist le hiomad guth agus le hiomad flosc cainte. Tháinig an freagra leis an iomadúlacht chéanna amhail is dá mba gur bhraith cách go gcaithfeadh siad labhairt ach go raibh srian éigin orthu scód a ligean leis na smaointe a bhí acu.

'Is é - is ea - ach mar sin!' arsa duine díobh go plobaisteach, agus ba léir go raibh cibé ciall a bhí aige tugtha ag an am sin.

'Mac tíre - ach ní mac tíre sa cheart!' arsa duine eile a raibh creathán ina ghlór.

'Ní haon mhaith bheith ag iarraidh é a lámhach gan an piléar beannaithe,' arsa an tríú duine, ach ar chuma i bhfad níos dírí.

'Orainn féin an milleán bheith amuigh oíche mar seo! Is maith mar atá ár gcuid míle marc saothraithe againn,' ón gceathrú duine.

'Bhí fuil ar leac an mharmair bhriste,' arsa duine eile fós tar éis meandair bhig—'níorbh í an tintreach a dhein an obair sin. Agus maidir leis siúd- an bhfuil sé slán? Breithnígí an scornach aige! Féach, a chairde, is amhlaidh go raibh an mac tíre ina luí air d'fhonn teas a choiméad ina chuid fola.'

Ghrinnigh an t-oifigeach mo scornach agus dúirt:

'Tá sé ceart go leor; níor polladh a chraiceann. Cad is brí leis seo go léir? Beag an seans go bhfaighimis é murach geonaíl an mhic tíre.'

'Cad d'imigh air?' d'fhiafraigh an fear a raibh mo cheann cuachta ina lámha aige. B'é ba lú den bhuíon ar fad a raibh eagla air, dar liom, mar bhí a dhá láimh socair gan chrith faoi mo cheann. Bhí comhartha mhionoifigigh ar a mhuinchille aige.

'D'imigh sé leis dá nead féin,' arsa an fear a raibh aghaidh fhada mhílítheach air, agus a raibh creathán sceimhle ina cholainn aige agus é ag féachaint mórthimpeall. 'Tá riar a ghnó d'uaigheanna istigh ansin dó le luí iontu. Seo libh a chairde - imímis go beo! Fágaimis an áit mhallaithe seo.'

Chuir an t-oifigeach im shuí mé, agus thug orduithe uaidh; ansin d'ardaigh roinnt fear ar muin chapaill mé. Léim sé ar an diallait ar mo chúl, chuir a lámha thart orm, agus dhein sméideadh orthu gluaiseacht; agus leis sin chuireamar ár dtóin leis na crainn agus d'imíomar linn go tapaidh in ord glan míleata.

Bhí mo theanga fós ina maide agus b'éigean dom fanacht im thost. Ní foláir nó gur thit mo chodladh orm; mar b'é an chéad chuimhne eile a tháinig chugam ná go rabhas im sheasamh agus saighdiúir mar thaca liom ar gach taobh díom. Bhí an lá geal nach mór chugainn, agus chonaic mé ga gréine uaim ó thuaidh mar a bheadh rian fola ina ruithneadh ar an sneachta bán. Bhí an t-oifigeach ag rá leo gan tada dá bhfaca siad a scaoileadh uathu, ach amháin go bhfaca siad strainséir de Shasanach, agus é arna chosaint ag madra ollmhór.

'Madra! Níorbh aon mhadra é sin,' arsa fear díobh a léirigh eagla cheana. 'Is dóigh liom go n-aithním mac tíre nuair a fheicim é.'

D'fhreagair an t-oifigeach go socair: 'Madra adúirt mé.'

'Madra!' arsa mo dhuine arís le teann íoróna. Ba léir go raibh a chuid misnigh ag éirí ar nós na gréine; agus ansin, ag síneadh méire im threo, dúirt, 'Féach leat a scornach. An ndéarfá gurb obair mhadra é sin, a mháistir!'

D'ardaigh mé mo lámh chun mo scornaí gan mhachnamh, agus nuair a theagmhaigh mé leis, ligeas uaill péine asam. Bhailigh na fir im thimpeall ag féachaint, cuid acu ag cromadh síos óna gcuid diallaití in airde; agus ansin arís chualamar glór socair ciúin an oifigigh óig:

'Madra, mar adúirt mé. Dá ndéarfaí rud ar bith eile bheimis inár gceap magaidh.'

Cuireadh um an am sin mé laistiar de thrúipéar, agus dheineamar marcaíocht go réidh chomh fada le bruach Munich amuigh. Is anseo a thángamar ar charráiste spárrtha inar cuireadh láithreach mé agus ghluaiseamar linn go dtí na Quatre Saisons. Rinne an t-oifigeach óg mé a thionlacan feadh an ama, fad is a bhí an trúipéar laistiar dínn lena chapall, agus d'imigh an chuid eile leo go dtí a gcuid beairicí.

Nuair a shroicheamar an áit tháinig Herr Delbrück ina ruathar na céimeanna síos ionas go raibh sé soiléir ar a iompar go raibh sé ag faire ón taobh istigh. Bheir sé greim ar mo dhá láimh go fonnmhar agus threoraigh isteach go caoin sochaideartha mé. Bheannaigh an t-oifigeach dom le comhartha saighdiúra agus bhí ar tí imeacht, nuair a d'aithin mé cad chuige a bhí sé, agus níorbh fholáir leis go dtiocfadh faram chun mo sheomra. Le linn dúinn gloine fíona a ól i bhfochair a chéile, ghabhas buíochas ó chroí leis agus lena chairde cróga ar son mé a thabhairt slán. Dúirt sé gur mó ná sásta a bhí sé féin, agus gurbh é Herr Delbrück a thóg an chéad chéim d'fhonn réiteach leis an díorma cuardaigh. Dhein an maître d'hotel miongháire de bharr an ráitis sin a bhféadfaí brí ar bith a bhaint as, agus d'imigh an t-oifigeach leis á rá go raibh dualgas éigin le comhlíonadh aige.

'Ach, a Herr Delbrück,' d'fhiosraigh mé, 'conas a tharla gur tháinig na saighdiúirí dom lorg in aon chor?'

Bhain sé searradh as a ghuaillí mar a bheadh lagmheas á chaitheamh aige ar a bheart féin, agus dúirt:

'Tharla an t-ádh a bheith liom go bhfuaireas cead imeachta ó cheannaire mo reisiminte féin chun lucht cuardaigh a fháil.'

'Ach conas a raibh fhios agat go rabhas ar iarraidh?'

'Tháinig an tiománaí chugainn abhus lena raibh fágtha aige dá charráiste a ndearnadh dochar dó nuair a theich a fhoireann capall.'

'Ach ná habair go gcuirfeá díorma cuardaigh amach faoi mo chomhairse amháin?'

'Ó, ní móide go ndéanfainn,' ar seisean, 'ach is amhlaidh go bhfuaireas an sreangscéal seo ón mBoyar úd a bhfuil tú mar aoi aige sul ar tháinig fear an charráiste chugainn.' Agus bhain sé an sreangscéal seo as a phóca aníos agus shín chugam é. Rinne mé é a léamh mar seo:

BISTRITZ

'Tabhair aire don aoi seo agam - is tábhachtach liom go dtiocfadh sé slán. Dá dtarlódh aon rud dó, nó dá rachadh sé ar iarraidh, déan níos mó ná do dhícheall chun é a aimsiú is a theasargan. Sasanach é agus dá bhrí sin tugtha don eachtraíocht. Is mó sin baol a leanann an sneachta agus na mac tírí istoíche. Ná

cuir soicind amú má cheapann tú gur tháinig aon dochar dó. Cúiteoidh mé do lándhíograis leat lena bhfuil de mhaoin shaolta agam. — Dracula.'

Nuair a bhí greim agam ar an sreangscéal i mo ghlaic, thosaigh an seomra ag déanamh bulla báisín im thimpeall; agus murach gur rug an maître d'hotel a bhí ar a aire orm is dóigh liom go raibh mé ar lár.

Bhí rud éigin chomh fíoraisteach sa chúrsa seo go léir, rud éigin chomh haduain agus deacair a shamhlú, gur tháinig aníos ionam an tuiscint go rabhas im bhreallán spóirt ag dhá fhórsa a bhí bunoscionn lena chéile. Ba leor meaththuairim lag mar seo ann féin chun stailc a dhéanamh díom. B'fhollas dom go rabhas faoi chosaint dhiamhair éigin. Tháinig scéala ó thír iasachta i bhfad uaim, go tráthúil ar éigean, scéala a thóg ó bhaol an tsuansneachta mé agus ó ghialla an mhic tíre in éineacht.

19. BRAM STOKER AND THE THEATRE

~ Leslie Shepard ~

If the name Bram Stoker means anything to people, it is usually only as the author of the immortal vampire thriller *Dracula*, which has had a tremendous influence on stage and screen all over the world since first publication in 1897.

But Stoker's dozen novels and his short stories were mostly spare time occupations during twenty-seven years devotion to the theatre as a manager to Sir Henry Irving until the great actor's death in 1905. This was more than a business arrangement, since Stoker remained Irving's greatest admirer and loyal friend throughout their association.

Stoker's lifelong devotion to the theatre was not surprising, since his father, Abraham Stoker (1799-1876), had also been a devoted theatregoer with an immense admiration for Edmund Kean, having seen all his Dublin performances. Stoker senior still went to the theatre occasionally in his seventies and his son took him to see Barry Sullivan as Sir Giles Overreach in Massinger's *A New Way To Pay Old Debts*.

Bram Stoker was born November 8, 1847, named after his father Abraham, but used the shortened form 'Bram' throughout his life. His birthplace at 15 The Crescent, Clontarf is still standing, although to date permission has not been granted for a plaque to be erected on the house. Opposite the house was a small park, at that time private, where residents could walk when the gate was unlocked. It was a magic, private world for childhood dreams, overlooking the endless panorama of Dublin Bay. In the Dracula Centenary year it was officially designated as 'Bram Stoker Park', open to the public. Bram had four brothers and two sisters; the eldest brother, William, later made a name for himself as a surgeon.

In November 1864 Bram entered Trinity College, Dublin, where he secured his B.A. & M.A. Although he had been a sickly child he was now an athletic giant and won many awards at Trinity for such sports as weight-lifting and walking. He joined the Philosophical Society and became president. His first paper to the Society (perhaps prophetically) was entitled *Sensationalism in Fiction and Society*. He later spoke on such varied topics as King Lear, Shakespeare's fools, Keats, Shelley and votes for women. The 'Phil' has preserved the minute books of that period which bear Bram's signature.

On his twenty-fifth birthday he became auditor of the Historical Society. A many-sided man, he championed the poetry of Walt Whitman, with whom he became a firm friend, and worked as a civil servant for ten tedious years at Dublin Castle (where he wrote his first book, *The Duties Of Clerks Of Petty Sessions In Ireland*).

In his spare time, he was an avid theatregoer, like his father, chiefly haunting the old Theatre Royal, where he saw such artists as Mr and Mrs Charles Mathews, Herman Vesin, Charles Dillon, T C King, Mr and Mrs Charles Kean and Barry Sullivan.

Bram first saw Henry Irving play in Sheridan's *The Rivals* at the Theatre Royal on August 28, 1867, and was immediately enchanted with Irving's performance as Captain Absolute. He wrote:

"What I saw, to my amazement and delight, was a patrician figure as real as the persons of one's dreams, and endowed with the same poetic grace. A young soldier, handsome, distinguished, self-dependent; compact of grace and slumbrous energy . . . Such a figure as could only be possible in an age when the answer to insolence was a sword thrust, when only those dare be insolent who could depend to the last on the heart and brain and arm behind the blade."

In his *Personal Reminiscences Of Henry Irving* (two vols, 1906), Bram recalled: "The acting of Henry Irving is, after nearly forty years, so vivid in my memory that I can recall his movements, his expressions, the tones of his voice." He commented bitterly on the absence of proper press notice of Irving. Many of the Dublin papers had no word at all of Irving's performances; others had brief and inept notices. A week after one play the *Irish Times* observed in small type: "Mr Irving and Mr Gaston Murray are painstaking and respectable artists."

Stoker did not see Irving again until May 1871, when the Vaudeville

Company presented James Albery's comedy, *Two Roses*, at the Theatre Royal, with Irving's outstanding characterisation of Digby Grant. Stoker went to the play three times during the fortnight's run; another young man in the audience was a fifteen year old clerk who would also be fascinated with theatre - his name was George Bernard Shaw.

In spite of the play's success, the Dublin papers did not say anything about Irving or even the supporting players. Stoker's indignation at this neglect led him to seek out Dr Henry Maunsell, editor of the *Dublin Evening Mail*, and beg to be allowed to write dramatic notices. Maunsell said that the paper could not afford to pay for it, so Stoker said he would gladly do it without fee. From November 1871 for five years he had a free hand and covered plays at the Theatre Royal, the Queens, and the Gaiety. In those days, the Mail went to press around midnight and it was usual for such notices to appear a day late, which was hardly helpful to actors making a limited appearance or playing a different production each night. Stoker started the innovation of preparing his notice and getting it in type within a couple of hours of the show. Naturally, as a novice reviewer, working at speed, his notices were often pedestrian and might vary from one paragraph for a pantomime to a whole column for a serious play, but his love of theatre was manifest. His reviews were not only unpaid, as a labour of love, but also unsigned.

About this time, Stoker read the powerful supernatural story, *Carmilla*, by another Dubliner, J. Sheridan Le Fanu. *Carmilla* is one of the great

masterpieces of vampire fiction. The story made a powerful impression on Stoker and clearly planted the seeds of his own thriller, *Dracula*, published over twenty years later. He felt an urge to write stories himself, but the unpaid reviews and his work as a clerk at Dublin Castle took up most of his time. His home life was beginning to break up. His eldest brother, William, was now teaching medicine, Tom had graduated and entered the Indian Civil Service. Bram's two youngest brothers were studying at a medical school. The parents were in debt and decided that they could live more cheaply abroad. They sold up the house and took Bram's two sisters with them to France, later moving to Switzerland. Bram was installed in an apartment at 30 Kildare Street, on the other side of the road to the National Library. In 1983, the Bram Stoker Society persuaded Dublin Tourism to erect a plaque on the house, and Stoker's granddaughter, Ann Stoker, performed the unveiling.

In 1875, Stoker found time to write lurid serials for *The Shamrock* magazine. "The Chain of Destiny", in four parts, was in the Gothic tradition with romance, an evil curse and a villain known as "the phantom of the fiend."

I should like to digress here for a moment on the nature of Gothic fiction and its connection with the stage. The genre had been launched in 1764 with the publication of Horace Walpole's *The Castle Of Otranto*, subtitled "A Gothic Story". It initiated a literary form of fantasy fiction, combining mystery, romance, supernaturalism and sentimentality in a setting of mock-medieval architecture - hence the term "Gothic".

A by-product of the Gothic romance was its adaptation to the stage, when hundreds of Gothic plays were produced, some based on popular Gothic romances, others specially written. M.G. Lewis, who secured a sensational success with his Gothic novel *The Monk* (3 vols, 1796), added to his reputation by a number of Gothic plays with elaborate melodramatic settings and special effects which taxed the machinery of the stage. It is interesting to note that J.R. Planche's Gothic play *The Vampire* (1820) first introduced the technical stage innovation of the "Vampire Trap", a new kind of trap-door.

There were adaptations of Mary Shelley's *Frankenstein*, and this marriage of Gothic romance with stage melodrama, which had its heyday from the end of the eighteenth century for some three or four decades, was something of a first run for the Hollywood horror cycle in modern times, often involving the same Gothic themes. Scores of plays and movies have proliferated from Bram Stoker's novel *Dracula*. One precursor of Stoker in this Gothic genre was the Irish writer Charles Maturin (1780 - 1824), author of the Gothic romance *Melmoth The Wanderer* (3 vols., 1820). Melmoth was produced on the stage in 1825, and Maturin was also responsible for other Gothic melodramas. Like Stoker and Sheridan Le Fanu, Maturin was a Trinity College graduate, and the Irish influence on the Gothic genre has been an important one.

Of course, the Gothic impulse of horror, supernaturalism and gloomy settings predated Walpole's *Castle Of Otranto*, and I think it would be fair to say that there were Gothic elements in Shakespeare and other Elizabethan dramatists like Webster and Tourneur. Shakespeare's *Macbeth* and *Hamlet* are surely in the Gothic genre, although with deeper emotions than Gothic sentimentality.

It was Irving's performance in *Hamlet* at the Theatre Royal in Dublin in 1876 that revived Stoker's admiration of five years earlier and resulted in a lifelong friendship. *Hamlet* had long been one of Irving's great triumphs at the Lyceum Theatre in London two years earlier in 1874. Even with second-hand scenery the play had attracted every kind of appreciative audience and became the talk of the town. Edward Russell wrote in the *Liverpool Daily Post* that Irving "has made Hamlet much more than a type of feeble doubt, of tragic struggle, or even of fine philosophy. The immortality of his Hamlet is immortal youth, immortal enthusiasm, immortal tenderness, immortal nature."

In Dublin, Stoker was electrified by Irving's Hamlet and in a review wrote:; "In his fits of passion there is a realism that no one but a genius can ever effect." He went to the play three times during its run and even wrote a second laudatory notice, in which he said: "The great, deep, underlying idea of Hamlet is that of a mystic . . . In the high-strung nerves of the man; in the natural impulse of spiritual susceptibility; in his concentrated action spasmodic that it sometimes be, and in the divine delirium of his perfected passion, there is the instinct of the mystic which he has but to render a little plainer, in order that the less susceptible senses of this audience may see and understand . . . Mr Irving deserves not only the highest praise that can be accorded, but the loving gratitude of all to whom his art is dear."

Irving was pleased by such praise and invited Stoker to his hotel for supper after the play. The next day, Irving invited him to dinner, and that evening commenced what Stoker described as "the close friendship between us which only terminated with his life - if indeed friendship, like any other form of love, can ever terminate." It was a truly memorable occasion. As Stoker described it years later: "Thus it was that on this particular night my host's heart was from the beginning something toward me, as mine had been toward him. He had learned that I could appreciate high effort; and with the instinct of his craft liked, I suppose, to prove himself again to his new, sympathetic and understanding friend. And so after dinner he said he would like to recite for me Thomas Hood's poem *The Dream Of Eugene Aram*. That experience I shall never - can never - forget . . . Here in a hotel drawing-room, amid a dozen friends, a man in evening dress stood up to recite a poem with which we had all been familiar from our schooldays, which most if not all or us had ourselves recited at some time. But such was Irving's commanding force, so great was the magnetism of his genius, so profound was the sense of his dominance that I sat spellbound."

Today that poem may seem to us mere melodramatic doggerel, with lines like:

> "One that had never done me wrong
> A feeble man and old
> I led him to a lonely field
> The moon shone clear and cold:
> Now here, said I, this man shall die
> And I will have his gold!"

Yet by some inner magic Irving transmuted such verses into a terrifying reality, and at the conclusion collapsed half fainting. Overwhelmed with deep emotion, Stoker sat silent for a few seconds then burst out into something like a hysterical fit. Equally moved, Irving went into his bedroom for a few minutes, then came out with a signed photograph of himself, with an inscription on the back, the ink still wet: "My dear friend Stoker. God bless you! God bless you!! Henry Irving. Dublin, December 3, 1876."

During that memorable visit to Dublin, Stoker organised two unique honours to Irving from Dublin University, both unofficial but entirely representative. The first was an Address presented in the dining hall by University graduates and under-graduates. Part of this address, drafted by Stoker was as follows:

"For the delight and instruction that we (in common with our fellow citizens) have derived from all your impersonations, we tender you our sincere thanks. But it is something more than gratitude for personal pleasure or personal improvement that moves us to offer this public homage to your genius. Acting such as yours ennobles and elevates the stage, and serves to restore it to its true function as a potent instrument for intellectual and moral culture. Throughout your too brief engagement our stage has been a school of true art, a purifier of the passions, and a nurse of heroic sentiments; you have even succeeded in commending it to the favour of a portion of society, large and justly influential, who usually hold aloof from the theatre."

Irving responded with a gracious acknowledgement, which included the following lines:

"I believe that this is one of the very rare occasions on which public acknowledgement has been given by an Academic body to the efforts of a player, and this belief impresses me with the magnitude of the honour which you have conferred . . . It is only natural in the presence of gentlemen whose Alma Mater holds such state among institutions of learning that I should feel embarrassed in the choice of words with which to thank you; but I beg you to believe this. For my Profession, I tender you gratitude; for my Art I honour you; for myself, I would that I could speak all that is in my soul. But I cannot; and so falteringly tender you my most grateful thanks."

The second honour, on December 11, 1876, was a "University Night", in which Trinity College took every seat in the theatre and allocated places for Fellows, Professors and other dignitaries, alumni and the undergraduates, who occupied the pit and gallery, five hundred places in all. All the university men wore crimson rosettes. Irving could not have played to a more enthusiastic audience. The performance was greeted with tempestuous applause, and, deeply moved, Irving made a curtain speech of gratitude. Afterwards, there were scenes which Dublin theatregoers had never witnessed before and which have never been seen since. As Stoker reported:

" . . . a vast crowd of young men, nearly all students, waited outside the stage door to escort the actor to his hotel, the Shelbourne, in St Stephen's Green. This they did in noble style. They had come prepared with a long, strong rope, and taking the horses from the carriage harnessed themselves to it. There were over a thousand of them, and as no more than a couple of hundred of them could get a hand on the rope, the rest surrounded us - for I accompanied my friend on that exciting progress - on either side a shouting body. The street was a solid moving mass and the wild uproar was incessant. To us the street was a sea of faces, for more than half the body were turning perpetually to have another look at the hero of the hour. Up Grafton Street we swept, the ordinary passengers in the street falling of necessity back into doorways and side streets; round into St Stephen's Green, where the shouting crowd stopped before the hotel. Then the cheering became more organised. The desultory sounds grew into more exact and recurring volume till the cheers rang out across the great square and seemed to roll away towards the mountains in the far distance.

Irving was greatly moved, almost overcome . . And so amid endless cheering and relentless hand-shaking, we forced a way into the hotel."

Over the next couple of years, the association between Irving and Stoker ripened. Whenever Irving came to Dublin, he would make time to meet Stoker, discuss plans, and dine with him. By now, Stoker had moved to an elegant apartment in Harcourt Street. Irving visited him there and discussed his future acting career, and threw out a hint that Stoker might join forces with him on management. Afterwards Stoker wrote enthusiastically in his diary, 22nd November, 1877, "London in view!" He had yearned to be associated with the stage ever since his earlier success in publishing his serial "The Chain of Destiny". At that period, he had taken a short holiday in Paris, where he met an actress whom he described only as "Miss Henry". He wrote to his father and said he wanted to write a play for the actress and even throw up his Civil Service job and become an author! His father was alarmed and pointed out that his job was a good one with prospects of promotion; he also warned gravely of association with actors and actresses: "Although I am ready to admit that in many instances their society was very agreeable, still I don't think they are altogether desirable acquaintances to those not connected with their own profession (if I may call it), because it may involve expense and other matters which are not at all times advantageous. Under the circumstances I believe such acquaintanceship is better avoided." At that time, the association with Miss Henry faded out rapidly, but not Stoker's passion for the theatre. He now had hopes that his close friendship with Irving would lead to a full-time theatrical post.

In 1878 Stoker had become deeply attached to Florence Balcombe, a beautiful girl who had been formerly courted by Oscar Wilde. Stoker had been a frequent visitor to the Wildes. Florence shared Stoker's love of music and theatre and seemed an ideal companion who would not stand in his way in his desire to work with Irving. In June, Stoker went to London to see Irving in the first night of the play *Vanderdecken* by an Irish playwright, W.G. Wills, based on the Flying Dutchman legend. Stoker commented on Irving's performance: "I think his first appearance was the most striking and startling thing I ever saw on stage." But Stoker felt that the play itself needed tightening up and spent the weekend with Irving cutting and altering the script. It was clear that the two men could work well together. Three months later, in September, Irving was back in Dublin for a fortnight, and between performances the two friends were inseparable.

Irving told Stoker how he planned to take over the Lyceum Theatre in London.

Only six weeks later Stoker received an urgent telegram asking him to come to Glasgow, where Irving was on tour, to discuss important business. The following evening Stoker was with Irving, who told him that he had leased the Lyceum and needed an acting manager - would Stoker take on the job? It was the turning point in Stoker's career for which he had longed. He accepted immediately, wired his resignation as a civil servant, and sent a telegram to Florence Balcombe. He had planned to get married the following year. Instead, the marriage took place at St Ann's in Dawson Street a few days later on December 4th. On December 9th, 1878, together with his wife, Stoker joined forces with Irving in Britain, an association that lasted throughout Irving's lifetime. Only Stoker's mother disapproved, commenting acidly: "Manager to a strolling player."

Soon after Stoker joined Irving, his first book, *The Duties Of Clerks Of Petty Sessions In Ireland*, was in print, a reminder of a life he had left behind.

Stoker was nominally acting manager, but as a close personal friend of Irving, he made unique contributions to Irving's career far beyond formal duties. In addition to organising and supervising all the complex behind-scenes activities, he was a confidante to the supporting players, and especially to Irving's famous co-star, Ellen Terry, who relied constantly on Stoker's advice and guidance. Stoker read plays sent to the company. He also dealt with Irving's large fan mail, wrote the star's letters for him, sometimes fifty a day. His background as a drama critic made his opinions on rehearsals or stage business valuable to the cast. He was public relations man, welfare officer, tour organiser. On Irving's spectacularly successful American tours, the organisation involved was phenomenal. The company sometimes involved over ninety people, filling a train, with ten baggage cars of costumes and properties, to be shepherded often through blizzards and snow several feet deep on a relentless schedule.

Although the company had a treasurer, it was Stoker who controlled the finances, no easy task in view of Irving's lavish life-style at the peak of his success. During Stoker's first year, the actor revived the old Beefsteak Club Room in the Lyceum Theatre, using it for supper parties after a production. The Sublime Society of Beefsteaks had been founded by John Rich, famous for his association with John Gay on *The Beggar's Opera* in 1735. Originally based in Covent Garden, it was an exclusive dining club, limited to twenty-four members, and even the Prince Regent in his time had to wait for a vacancy before he could join. The Club became the centre for the leading authors, wits and aristocracy of the day until dissolved in 1867. Irving revived much of the Club's former glory by lavish entertainment. When the guests exceeded the thirty-six who could be accommodated in the Beefsteak Room, the stage itself was turned into a supper room. The first night gatherings on the stage of the Lyceum after a play could have been a Who's Who of the great and famous of the day.

One of the guests at the Beefsteak Room on April 30, 1890, was the famous traveller Arminius Vambéry, who had come to see Irving in *The Dead Heart* by Watts Phillips with a plot similar to Charles Dickens' *A Tale Of Two Cities*. Vambéry was from Budapest and told many thrilling stories about his adventures. Stoker met him again at Dublin University, when Vambéry was given an honorary degree. It was Vambery who supplied Stoker with background information on Transylvania and the history of Wallachia, which was the starting point for Stoker's thriller **Dracula**, based on a real life tyrant of the fifteenth century.

It is amazing that Stoker ever found time to write several novels and a number of short stories in between his strenuous duties as Irving's manager. His work at the Lyceum made great demands on his time and energy. He would be at the theatre every morning, then spend a few hours with his wife and young son before returning to the Lyceum for the evening performances. Afterwards, he might be needed for managerial conferences or to organise the sumptuous suppers for Irving's guests, getting back to his wife and child in the early hours of the morning. Sunday was his only free day, and in between demanding tours, he would take a fortnight's holiday.

Under the circumstances, his literary performance was almost as remarkable as Irving's theatrical progress. It is obvious that *Dracula* alone must have required a considerable amount of detailed research, spread over several years. The seventy-eight pages of working notes for the book in the collection of the Rosenbach Museum and Library in Philadelphia show that Stoker consulted coastguard logbooks on ship sailings, manuals about barometers, wind changes, cloud signs, storms and local colour at Whitby, researched clothing, agriculture and folklore of the Carpathian mountains, checked with his brother William about the precise details of wounds and other medical details.

The book was published in June 1897 and became a sensational best-seller; it has been in print ever since. Within only a few days of publication, Stoker presented a stage version at the Lyceum. This play was little more than a hastily contrived reading as copyright performance, in order to protect the plot and dialogue from piracy. There was a prologue, five acts with a total of forty-seven scenes, and a cast of fifteen. Posters were put up only half an hour before the performance, which was watched only by friends and the theatre cleaners. Irving must have watched this impromptu drama with amused superiority. When Stoker asked him what he thought of it, he replied dismissively: "Dreadful!"

The play was never repeated in Stoker's lifetime, although a young Irish actor named Hamilton Deane, who joined the Henry Irving Vacation Company in 1899, thought the story had wonderful stage possibilities. Deane met Stoker but never had an opportunity to discuss the project. After Stoker's death he was a star on Broadway, New York. He carried the novel *Dracula* around with him on his travels, but it was not until 1923 that Deane himself wrote the standard play version, first presented at the Grand Theatre, Derby, in June 1924. Deane acquired sole dramatic rights from Stoker's widow, Florence. The play was an instant success and played to packed houses for years afterwards. As Deane himself commented: "We never had a poor house with 'Dracula'. By that time I was simply coining money with the play. I could not go wrong with it anywhere." In 1939 Deane himself took the title role in a performance at the Lyceum Theatre, where Irving had dismissed the original version as "dreadful". The film star, Bela Lugosi, famous for his performance in the first American movie version of *Dracula* (directed by Tod Browning in 1931), walked on stage one night and warmly embraced Deane. It is interesting to note in passing that Lugosi's interpretation of the role received copyright protection as late as 1972, when the Superior Court in California, in the case of *Lugosi et al. -v- Universal Pictures Company Inc. et al.* held that Lugosi and even his heirs had an enforceable "right of publicity" in his name, his face and his various characterisations!

Lugosi was perhaps the most famous Dracula of the screen, but the Tod Browning movie of 1931 was not the first screen version. Film enthusiasts will know that there was an unauthorised silent film version titled *Nosferatu*, directed by F.W. Murnau in 1921. Stoker's widow, Florence, prosecuted the film-makers for infringement of copyright, but in spite of a court order in 1925 to destroy all negatives and prints, copies somehow reached America, where the film was released in 1929 under the title *Nosferatu The Vampire*. Elsewhere, until recently, the film was shown only to film societies and other specialised audiences. The Bram Stoker Society showed a video copy of the film in 1984. Many people believe that *Nosferatu* was a far superior and imaginative version of the story than the Hollywood film of 1931 with Bela Lugosi, and there was a lovingly reverent remake of *Nosferatu* by the German director, Werner Herzog, in 1979, recreating the original settings and story with all the added impact of modern cinematic skill.

It is strange to reflect that Stoker's thriller *Dracula* has eclipsed the memory of Irving's performances, and probably had a greater influence on drama, especially in the scores of films and plays which have stemmed from it, together with a considerable body of scholarly and exegetical literature. Stoker always gave first place in his energies and affections to the theatre of Henry Irving, and had urged that Irving be granted a knighthood as early as 1883. Irving accepted the honour in 1895, the first actor to be knighted.

It cannot be doubted that Irving had genius as an actor, but equally his success over so many years owed much to the devotion, loyalty and

generosity of his friend and lieutenant, Bram Stoker. For the triumphs and heartbreaks of the twenty-seven years with Irving, it is useful to read Stoker's *Personal Reminiscences Of Henry Irving* (2 vols, 1906), but you will have to read between the lines to realise Stoker's tremendous sacrifices over the years. There is not a single word of criticism of his idol Irving, nor any indication of the undoubted fact that Irving often treated him very shabbily. It has been suggested that Stoker's wife, Florence, was frigid and that she remained aloof from Bram after the birth of their son, Noel, but the truth is surely that Stoker was married to his work with Irving and spent less time with his own wife. It is tempting to speculate that the vampiric character of Stoker's *Dracula* was unconsciously modelled on the insatiable temperament of Irving himself, totally demanding of vitality and loyalty.

There is often a melodramatic air to much of Stoker's writing, which shows how deeply he was inspired by the stage and by the performances of Irving in such emotionally charged productions as *Eugene Aram* or *The Bells*. Irving was certainly autocratic, self-centred, ruthless and totally absorbed by his own image and career. Nobody knew this better than Ellen Terry, who once remarked: "Yes, yes, were I to be run over by a steam-roller tomorrow, Henry would be deeply grieved; and would say quietly 'what a pity!', and then add after a moment or two's reflection, 'Who is there - er - to go on for her tonight?"

When Irving planned his second American tour in 1884 he decided to make his own schedule and wrote: "Our return tour will exceed this present one, I am certain, and I shall be my own manager - and have no middle man." He had engaged a secretary named Louis Frederick Austin, who made no secret of his dislike for Stoker, whom he attempted to supplant as Irving's right-hand man. He intrigued with Irving on the second American tour, mocking Stoker's literary talent, which he called 'blarneying', and even supplanted him in writing speeches for Irving. Stoker must have been deeply hurt by such treachery, but there is not a single word of criticism in his *Reminiscences*.

Over the years of extravagant spending and lavish entertainment by Irving, Stoker skilfully nursed the finances and tried to keep off bankruptcy. Irving's hospitality was endless. On the 100th night of *The Merchant of Venice* on February 14, 1880, there were 350 guests. In 1896, on the 25th anniversary of Irving's performance of *The Bells* at the Lyceum, there was a stage supper for 500 guests. During the 1890s Irving took a house with an enormous garden at Brook Green, Hammersmith, and once announced to Stoker that he wanted to give a garden party for his friends and acquaintances. Stoker worked on the list, then finally reported that it would not be possible. He held up his sheets of paper and said "There are too many!" Irving exclaimed: "Oh, nonsense, my dear fellow. You forget it is a huge garden." Stoker brandished his list and replied: "The other is huger. I am not half way through yet and they total up already over five thousand!"

In February 1898, Irving's career suffered its greatest setback with the disastrous fire at the Lyceum storage warehouses, which destroyed properties and 2,000 pieces of scenery from 42 plays. It was a catastrophic loss of more than £30,000 in value - apart from the impossibility of replacing scenery which would have taken years to construct. To make matters worse, Irving had earlier insisted on reducing the insurance cover to cut down on expenses. Stoker had to face the reporters and put a bold face on it. They still had costumes, the scenery could be reconstructed, and the theatre need not close, he claimed. Asked, "What does Sir Henry say?" he replied, "He bears it calmly." In fact, Irving sulked and left it to Stoker to sort out the mess and head off financial collapse by skilful management.

Ellen Terry commented of Irving: "For years he has accepted favours, obligations to, etc. through Bram Stoker. Never will he acknowledge them himself, either by businesslike receipt or by any word or sign. He 'lays low' like Brer Rabbit better than anyone I have ever met." Stoker himself wrote of that dreadful period: "There was strict reticence on financial matters. No one official of the theatre, outside myself, knew the whole of the incomings and outgoings. Not even that official designated 'Treasurer' knew anything of the high finance of the undertaking."

Not surprisingly, the end of the season saw a loss, and in October 1898 Irving went down with pleurisy and pneumonia for seven weeks. When he recovered, he seemed to resent his dependence on Stoker, who had prepared a rational rescue plan for the company finances. Irving never liked to economise. While convalescing at Bournemouth, he went behind Stoker's back and signed away the Lyceum to a syndicate on unfavourable conditions. Stoker did his best to get better terms, and to keep the Lyceum going under difficult conditions.

By now, Irving was in his final years and not in the best of health. But he struggled on, even undertaking two more six-month tours in America at the age of sixty-one. His star was falling. A newer school of drama criticism claimed he was old-fashioned, and George Bernard Shaw never missed an opportunity to be spiteful about Irving.

Now there were further serious financial problems. In 1902, the London County Council demanded costly alterations to the Theatre to meet safety requirements. Stoker returned from a tour with Irving in Manchester to find a shareholders' meeting to consider turning the Lyceum into a music-hall! Irving was blamed for the financial fiasco, but Stoker made an impassioned speech in his defence, pointing out that Irving had made great personal sacrifices and given up his lease of the theatre, as well as losing a great deal of his own money. The shareholders cheered Irving, but it did not save the Lyceum, which closed its doors.

Irving was now without his own theatre, and Ellen Terry was no longer in the company. After his last American tour in 1903, Irving planned to make just two more provincial tours and then retire, but he collapsed at Wolverhampton in spring 1905. Ellen Terry went to see him and brought flowers. They talked of old times and both knew that the end was near. Irving's doctor had warned him that his constitution would not stand the intense strain of another performance of *The Bells*. Yet he rallied sufficiently to give a fine performance in *Becket* at the Drury Lane Theatre in London, and finally at the Theatre Royal, Bradford, in October. He was warmly applauded by an enthusiastic audience who did not want to leave the theatre. Afterwards, in the dressing room, Stoker said; "Now that you're rid of the fear of having to play *The Bells* you'll be yourself again soon. You're getting back into the old stride."

As they parted, Irving suddenly made an unaccustomed affectionate gesture, grasping Stoker by the hand. "Muffle up your throat, old chap," he said, "It's bitterly cold tonight and you have a cold. Take care of yourself. Goodnight, God bless you." A few hours later, Stoker was summoned urgently to Irving's hotel. The actor had fainted in the hall and died two minutes before Stoker arrived. It was a sad, dramatic final curtain.

Irving's death was a bitter blow, after the final years of ill health and financial worry, and Stoker was grief-stricken at the loss of his old friend. He suffered a stroke and was unconscious for twenty-four hours, then ill for many weeks.

But he struggled on with his own writing. Over the next few years he published more novels: *The Man, Lady Athlyne, The Lady Of The Shroud, The Lair Of The White Worm*, a volume of short stories titled *Snowbound*, a collection of real-life mysteries titled *Famous Impostors*, as well as many magazine articles. His *Personal Reminiscences Of Henry Irving* (2 vols, 1906) was a glowing tribute to his friend's genius as an actor, and underplayed his own part in the actor's success. He knew that Irving had been widely criticised for his extravagance and self-interest, but refused to echo such judgments. He wrote, with typical generosity: "For my own part, my love and admiration for Irving were such that nothing I could tell to others - nothing that I can recall to myself - could lessen his worth. I only wish that, so far as I can achieve it, others now or hereafter may see him with my eyes. For well I know that if they do, his memory shall not lack. He was a man with all a man's weaknesses and mutabilities as well as a man's strong qualities. Had he not had in his own nature all the qualities of natural man how could he have for close on half a century embodied such forces - general and distinctive - in such a long series of histrionic characters whose fidelity to natural type became famous."

Stoker's last article, published in the *Nineteenth Century* magazine, May 1911, was titled "Irving and Stage Lighting" and sought to show how Irving had pioneered the art of stage lighting. Soon afterwards, Stoker died, on April 20, 1912, at the age of sixty-four.

There have been recent rumours that the death certificate cause of 'Locomotor Ataxy 6 months Granular Contracted Kidney. Exhaustion' somehow implied syphilis, and a reckless mythology has been circulated that, in company with Irving, Stoker might have consorted with prostitutes. This is mischievous speculation and wholly out of character. Irving himself devoted all his energies to acting and his own marriage had broken up quite early on that account. Stoker's steadfast code of loyalty, honour and chivalry would be totally opposed to casual sex. Whatever energy he had left after twenty-seven gruelling years with Irving was surely sublimated in his thrillers. The one revealing word on the death certificate is 'Exhaustion'. Like his friend Irving, Stoker worked himself to death.

Irving was, of course, a great actor but it cannot be doubted that Stoker was the driving force behind his successful career. The politician, Henry Labouchere, stated: "Had it not been for his old friend Bram Stoker, Irving would have been eaten out of home and theatre very speedily." Ellen Terry commented: "He filled a difficult position with great tact, and was not so universally abused as most business managers, because he was always straight with the company, and never took a mean advantage of them."

It is sad that Stoker's important work for theatre for more than a quarter century has now been eclipsed by the newer medium of cinema. The old Theatre Royal where Stoker was transported by the performances of Irving was destroyed by fire in 1880. Twice rebuilt, it finished up in 1935 with programmes of music hall variety, and film shows.

Stoker's encouragement of enlightened theatregoing in Dublin has been forgotten in his own country. There are no more expressions of mass enthusiasm for theatre such as Stoker organised for Irving in 1876. A modern generation now flocks in its thousands to rock music festivals. The Theatre Royal was demolished in 1962 to make way for a modern office block.

20. OBITUARY OF BRAM STOKER

Times, April 22, 1912 – Obituary

Bram Stoker

The death took place at 26, St.George's Square, S.W., after a long illness, of Mr. Bram Stoker, who for nearly 30 years was the intimate friend of Sir Henry Irving. Mr. Stoker had been ill since 1906.

Bram, or baptismally Abraham Stoker, was born in Dublin in 1847, his father Abraham being one of the officials in the Chief Secretary's Department at the Castle. He was educated at Trinity College, where he won honours in science, mathematics, oratory, history, and composition, besides distinguishing himself as a sportsman and debater. He was for some time in the Irish Civil Service as Inspector of Petty Sessions, and was engaged in journalism as well, being editor of an evening paper and as a dramatic critic. How long he would have been content to play these humble though miscellaneous parts it is impossible to tell; but in 1876 or thereabouts he first came into contact with Henry Irving, and two years later he had permanently thrown in his lot with him as his manager and confidential secretary, and he remained with him until the end. Few men have played their part of *fidus achates* to a great personality with more gusto. Mr. Stoker must have found his new life thoroughly congenial. He shared Irving's counsels in all his enterprises; went about with him in the closest relationship as confidential secretary and right-hand man; assisted in many brilliant entertainments which his chief gave during the heyday of the Lyceum; met and was cordially treated by people of all sorts and conditions; and knew thoroughly the ins and outs of the financial side of the riskiest of all professions. From 1878, the year in which Irving became lessee and manager of the Lyceum, to 1905; when he died, the takings, as Stoker tells us, exceeded two millions. When the crash came, Stoker remained loyally at his friend's side, during the years which would have been fatal to less enduring spirits. After Irving's death, it was not annatural that Stoker should write his biography, and this task Mr. Stoker presented with his customary enthusiasm. A fluent and flamboyant writer, with a manner and mannerisms which faithfully reflected the mind which moved the pen, Stoker managed to find time amid much arduous and distracting work, to write a good deal. He was a master of a particularly florid and creepy kind of fiction, represented by "Dracula" and other novels. He had also essayed musical comedy, and had of late years resumed his old connection with journalism. But his chief literary memorial with all its extravagances and shortcomings - Mr. Stoker was no very acute critic of his chief as an actor - cannot but remain a valuable record of the workings of genius as they appeared to his devoted associate and admirer.

Mr. Bram Stoker married Florence Anne Lemon, daughter of the late Lieutenant-Colonel Balcombe, who survives him with one son, Noel Thornley.

The funeral is to take place quietly at Golder's Green.

Times, April 25, 1912

The funeral of Mr. Bram Stoker took place yesterday [24th] at the Golder's Green Crematorium. A service was held in the chapel by the Rev. Herbert Trundle. Among those present were Mr. Lawrence Irving, Mr. Hall Caine, Mr. Ford Maddox Hueffer and Miss Genevive Ward. Wreaths were sent by Miss Ellen Terry, Sir Athur Pinero, Mrs. Maxwell, and Mr. and Mrs. Frederick Watson.

(Photograph: John Exshaw)

Certificate of Death.

PURSUANT TO THE BIRTHS AND DEATHS REGISTRATION ACTS, 1836 to 1874.

Registration District: ST. GEORGE, HANOVER SQUARE.

DEATH in the Sub-District of BELGRAVE, in the County of LONDON.

When and Where Died.	Name and Surname.	Sex.	Age.	Rank or Profession.	Cause of Death.	Signature, Description, and Residence of Informant.	When Registered.	Signature of ...
Twentieth April 1912. 26 St. George's Square.	Abraham Stoker	Male	64 Years	Author	Locomotor Ataxy 6 Month. Granular Contracted Kidney, Exhaustion. Certified by James Browne M.D.	present at the death W. Thornley Stoker Sn. 5 Fernshaw Mansions Chelsea.	Twenty second April 1912.	Registrar

I, LOUIS CHARLES MOUNSTEPHEN, Registrar of Births and Deaths for the Sub-District of BELGRAVE, in the County of LONDON, DO HEREBY CERTIFY that this is a true ...

Entry No. 298 ... in the Register Book of Deaths for the said Sub-District, and that such Register Book is now legally in my custody.

WITNESS my hand, this Twenty second day of April 1912.

Louis C. Mounstephen, Registrar.

21. A NOTE ON THE DEATH CERTIFICATE OF BRAM STOKER

~ Leslie Shepard ~

In the last few years, a reckless mythology alleges that Bram Stoker died of syphilis There are two sources for this story. The main source is Daniel Farson, great-nephew of Stoker, in his book *The Man Who Wrote Dracula* (London, 1975; New York, 1976). A secondary source is a family tradition of Senator David Norris, a connection of the Dublin city branch of the Stoker family. Farson's claim rests on the interpretation of the Death Certificate of Stoker, which reads: 'Locomotor Ataxy 6 months, Granular Contracted Kidney, Exhaustion.' Farson asserts that 'Locomotor Ataxy' is a euphemism for *Tabes Dorsalis* or General Paralysis of the Insane, the final stages of syphilis Senator Norris was under the impression that Stoker 'died of the pox', but this belief may derive from the Death Certificate as well as gossip amongst ancestors scandalised by the sensationalism of Stoker's novel *Dracula*. Dublin gossip is often hurtful and scandalous, as well as witty Since Bram Stoker died in London, the Death Certificate could well have been the source of this gossip. Farson's surprisingly emphatic interpretation of the Death Certificate of his relative rests on the common medical identification of 'Locomotor Ataxy' with the final stage of syphilis, but this is by no means invariable. I consulted a medical lecturer at the Wellcome Institute for the History of Medicine, who stated as follows :

'As for 'Locomotor Ataxy', it usually, (one can never put it more strongly than that) refers to the consequences of cerebellum disease due to tertiary syphilis. There is therefore a definite indication that syphilis is related to cause of death, but one can not be certain.'

This cautious statement confirms that there is no definite justification for assuming syphilis, and the circumstances surrounding Stoker's later years would seem to militate against the possibility. *Tabes Dorsalis* is usually the culmination of several years physical deterioration and brain damage, expressed in disturbances of vision, palsy, disorientation in walking, accompanied by mental degeneration. In the case of Stoker, he did not exhibit the mental deterioration that might be characteristic of General Paralysis of the Insane, since he was mentally alert and active with literary work almost up to his death in 1912 The fact that he had some muscular disorientation described as 'locomotor ataxy' is hardly surprising, since nine years earlier he had suffered a severe stroke after the death of his friend and idol Henry Irving. As Stoker's biographer Harry Ludlam wrote: 'He suffered a stroke which laid him unconscious for twenty-four hours, and which began a painful illness that dragged on for weeks, robbing his robust frame of much of its boundless vitality and leaving his eyesight impaired.' In the following years, however, Stoker revised his novel *The Man*, corrected proofs of his biography of Irving, and published five other books: *Lady Athlyne* (1908), *Snowbound* (1908), *The Lady of the Shroud* (1909), *Famous Impostors* (1910), *The Lair of the White Worm* (1911), as well as a number of articles in periodicals. None of this is characteristic of a man in the final stages of syphilis! Some physical difficulties were inevitable. He had struggled for years with overwork. The aftermath of the stroke in late life, coupled with earlier suffering from Bright's Disease and gout, could be expected to result in a condition of *paralysis agitans* or palsy, affecting his gait The really significant cause of death is surely the single word 'Exhaustion'.

22. BRAM STOKER'S DUBLIN

~ Leslie Shepard ~

Long after the death of Stoker in 1912, the tourist potential of locales associated with him is now being slowly recognised. In England, the Dracula Society was one of the first organisations to develop tourist interest in Transylvania (Romania), although Stoker had never been there but only described it accurately in *Dracula* through careful research. Under the guidance of Bruce Wightman and Bernard Davies, a tour package of Romania was organised successfully in 1983. This included following the route of Jonathan Harker in 'The Land Beyond the Forest' in Stoker's book. Bernard Davies also issued an excellent and scholarly description of this route in a booklet, which showed how accurately Stoker had researched the area. In subsequent years, similar tours became something of an annual pilgrimage for members of the Dracula Society, and stimulated other tourist agencies to promote similar packages.

The Dracula Society also pioneered visits to Whitby, Yorkshire, another

No.15 Marino Crescent, the birthplace of Stoker

Trinity College, as it looked at the turn of the century

important locale in Stoker's novel, and interested Scarborough Borough Council in issuing a leaflet *Whitby Dracula Trail*, charted by Bernard Davies. Whitby also developed a waxwork exhibition entitled *The Dracula Experience*.

In London, many visitors familiar with Stoker's book have been fascinated by Highgate Cemetery, believed to be associated with Dracula, and later the subject of controversial claims of real vampire hauntings in modern times. Two publications deal with these claims: *The Highgate Vampire* by Sean Manchester (1986) and *Beyond the Highgate Vampire* by David Farrant (1991). Another London locale is Stoker's house at 26 George's Square, which bears a commemorative plaque. Stoker was cremated at Golders Green Crematorium, where there is a memorial urn.

Surprisingly, the Irish associations of Stoker have received little attention. Yet Stoker was a Dublin man and published his earliest writings there. It was in Dublin that Stoker first witnessed the performances of Henry Irving at the Theatre Royal, and formed the friendship that was to result in becoming Irving's Manager for twenty-seven years. Ireland was also the home of two other significant writers of Gothic literature — Charles Maturin (1780-1824) and J. Sheridan Le Fanu (1814 - 1873). Like Stoker, they both attended Trinity College Dublin.

It is now surely time that Ireland was placed firmly on the map for tourism, with special Dublin tourist trails.

The Dublin associations with Stoker are rich in history. The elegant eighteenth century Marino Crescent where he was born was originally built by Charles Folliott as a 'spite fence', to block the view of Lord Charlemont of Marino House in Clontarf, after Folliott had quarrelled with his lordship.

In addition to No 15 being the birthplace of Stoker, it also housed the stolen Russian Crown Jewels, at one time the subject of negotiations between Soviets and Eamonn de Valera and Gerry Boland. The Boland family with strong Fianna Fáil political connections, also lived for a time at No. 15.

At No. 1 lived the Balcombe family whose daughter Florence married Stoker. The novelist William Carleton lived at No. 23 during the 1850's.

Much of Trinity College, Dublin, where Stoker took his B.A. and M.A. has changed since his time, but the Philosophical Society, now housed with the Historical Society in the Graduates Memorial Building, has preserved the minute books in which Stoker wrote his reports, signed 'A. Stoker'. The spacious and elegant debating chamber, which echoed wit and

Dublin Castle, as it was when Bram worked there

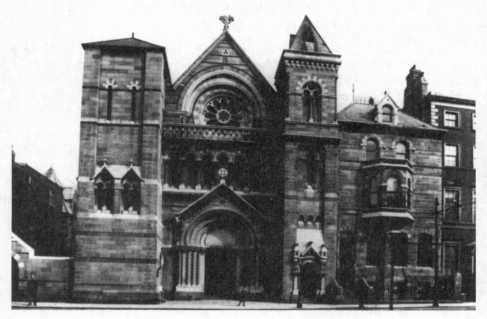

St. Ann's Church, Dawson Street, Dublin

erudition, is well worth a visit.

Dublin Castle still has many historic buildings, and there are guided tours of the sumptuous State Apartments. This ancient Castle had a troubled history, and during the sixteenth century the severed heads of rebels were impaled from the battlements in a manner reminiscent of the Transylvanian Dracula Vlad Tepes. The Petty Sessions Office in the Castle complex was located at No. 1 Exchange Court, since sold by the Office of Public Works for redevelopment as private dwellings. After Stoker's time it was moved to the Four Courts building on Ormond Quay, but the records were largely destroyed during the struggle for Irish Independence in 1922, when the building was shelled and set on fire.

Bram's eldest brother Sir William Thornley Stoker, the successful surgeon, lived in style at the superbly elegant Ely House in the city centre, later the home of the Knights of Columbanus.

In Dawson Street is St. Ann's Church where Stoker married Florence Balcombe; the poetess Felicia Hemans is buried here. Nearby in St. Stephen's Green is the stylish Shelbourne Hotel, where Henry Irving stayed during his Dublin tours, and where he was brought in triumph from the Theatre Royal in Hawkins Street through Grafton Street by students hitched to his carriage. Although the theatre was demolished in 1962 to make way for a new office block, the Gaiety Theatre, in South King Street, where Irving also played, is still standing.

Nearby, opposite the National Library in Kildare Street at No. 30, is a plaque commemorating Stoker's first independent address after his family home was sold up and his parents moved abroad. He later moved to Harcourt Street. Stoker is also featured in the Irish Writer's Museum established in Parnell Square, Dublin by Bord Fáilte to celebrate Cultural Capital Year in 1991.

Perhaps the strangest association with the Stoker family is to be found at the ancient church of St. Michan, a seventeenth century structure on the site of a Danish church dating back to 1195. This is located in Church Street, near the Four Courts building. It has a memorial tablet to the patriot Robert Emmet in the churchyard, although there is no evidence that his remains lie here. An early branch of the Stoker family owned one of the many underground vaults here. Through some curious feature of the atmosphere (perhaps a peat site, or limestone), there are centuries-old 'mummified' bodies in the vaults, which may be seen on a guided tour of this historic church, where the great composer G.F. Handel once played the organ.

The old Protestant church in Clontarf, where Stoker was baptised

Did Stoker know about these eerie vaults? It seems possible, since his brother Sir William once had a researcher list the seventeenth century members of the Stoker family, many associated with St. Michan's.

Bram Stoker himself was cremated at Golders Green Crematorium, north-west London, while his parents died abroad. But the 'mummified' bodies in St. Michan's are a curious foreshadowing of the Gothic theme of gloomy vaults and the Undead which became a feature of the Dracula myth.

(Photographs: The Leslie Shepard Bram Stoker Collection,
Dublin Writers' Museum)

BIBLIOGRAPHY

- Bingham, Madeleine (1978).
  Henry Irving and the Victorian Theatre   London: Allen and Unwin

- Dalby, Richard (1983).
  Bram Stoker; a Bibliography of First Editions   London: Dracula Press

- Farson, Daniel (1975).
  The Man Who Wrote Dracula   London: Michael Joseph

- Leatherdale, Clive (1985).
  Dracula; The Novel and The Legend   Wellingborough: Aquarian Press

- Ludlam, Harry (1962).
  A Biography of Dracula; The Life Story of Bram Stoker London: W. Foulsham

- McIntyre, Dennis (1987).
  The Meadow of the Bull; A History of Clontarf   Dublin

- Stoker, Bram (1897).
  Dracula   London: Archibald Constable & Co

  Frequently reprinted, recently available in the World's Classics Series, Oxford University Press (paperback), 1983, and (together with *The Lair of the White Worm*) in a *Bram Stoker Omnibus Edition*, W. Fousham, London, 1986. Dracula has also recently been reprinted by Penguin Classics (1993 ed. Maurice Hindle.)

- Stoker, Bram (1906).
  Personal Reminiscences of Henry Irving 2 vols.   London: W. Heinemann

- Wolf, Leonard (1975).
  The Annotated Dracula   New York: Clarkson N. Potter

THE DRACULA FILMS

Film	Year	featuring	Directed by
Nosferatu	1922	Max Schreck	F. W. Murnau
Dracula	1931	Bela Lugosi	Tod Browning
Dracula (Spanish Language Version)	1931	Carlos Villarias	George Melford
Mark Of The Vampire	1935	Bela Lugosi	Tod Browning
Dracula's Daughter	1936	Gloria Holden	Lambert Hillyer
Son Of Dracula	1943	Lon Chaney Jr.	Robert Siodmak
Return Of The Vampire	1943	Bela Lugosi	Lew Landers
House Of Frankenstein	1944	John Carradine	Erle C. Kenton
House Of Dracula	1945	John Carradine	Erle C. Kenton
Abbott And Costello Meet Frankenstein	1948	Bela Lugosi	Charles Barton
Drakula Instabulda	1953	Alif Captan	Mehmet Muhtar
The Return Of Dracula	1958	Francis Lederer	Paul Landres
Dracula or The Horror Of Dracula	1958	Christopher Lee	Terence Fisher
Brides Of Dracula	1960	David Peel	Terence Fisher
Kiss Of The Vampire	1963	Noel Willman	Don Sharp

Dracula - Prince Of Darkness *or* **Blood For Dracula**	1965	*Christopher Lee*	Terence Fisher
Billy The Kid Versus Dracula	1966	*John Carradine*	William Beaudine
A Taste Of Blood *or* **The Secret Of Dr. Alucard**	1967	*Bill Rogers*	Herschell Gordon Lewis
Dracula Has Risen From The Grave	1968	*Christopher Lee*	Freddie Francis
Blood Of Dracula's Castle	1969	*Alex D'Arcy*	Al Adamson
Jonathan, Vampire Sterben Nicht	1970	*Paul Albert Krumm*	Hans Geissendorfer
The Master Of The Dungeon	1970	*Des Roberts*	Laurence Merrick
The Heiress Of Dracula *or* **The Strange Adventure Of Jonathan Harker**	1970	*Susann Korda*	Jess Franco
Count Dracula *or* **El Conde Dracula**	1970	*Christopher Lee*	Peter Sasdy
Taste The Blood Of Dracula	1970	*Christopher Lee*	Peter Sasdy
Scars Of Dracula	1970	*Christopher Lee*	Roy Ward
Lake Of Dracula *or* **Chi O Suu Mi**	1971	*Shigen Amachi*	Michio Yamamoto
Dracula AD 1972	1972	*Christopher Lee*	Alan Gibson
Blacula	1972	*Charles McCauley*	William Crain
Countess Dracula	1972	*Ingrid Pitt*	Peter Sasdy
The Satanic Rites of Dracula	1973	*Christopher Lee*	Alan Gibson
Dracula *or* **Bram Stoker's Dracula**	1973	*Jack Palance*	Dan Curtis
Scream, Blacula Scream	1973	*William Marshall*	Bob Kelljan

Dracula's Saga *or* **La Saga De Los Draculas**	1973	*Narciso Ibañez Menta*	Leon Klimovsky
Countess Dracula *or* **The Devil's Wedding Night**	1975	*Sara Bey*	Roger Corman
Blood For Dracula	1975	*Udo Kier*	Paul Morrisey
Dracula: Father And Son *or* **Dracula: Pere et Fils**	1977	*Christopher Lee*	Edouard Molinaro
Tender Dracula *or* **Tendre Dracula**	1977	*Peter Cushing*	Pierre Grunstein
Nosferatu – Phantom Der Nacht	1979	*Klaus Kinski*	Werner Herzog
Dracula	1979	*Frank Langella*	John Badham
Countess Dolingen Of Gratz *or* **Les Jeux De La Comtesse Dolingen de Gratz**	1981	*Catherine Mathilde*	Catherine Binet
The Hunger	1983	*Catherine Deneuve*	Tony Scott
Bram Stoker's Dracula	1992	*Gary Oldman*	Francis F. Coppola
Vampire in Brooklyn	1995	*Eddie Murphy*	Wes Craven
Dracula – Dead and Loving It	1996	*Leslie Neilsen*	Mel Brooks

BOOKS ABOUT BRAM STOKER

There are hundreds of books concerned with Dracula, Vlad Tepes, Transylvania, etc, as well as scholarly theses and academic papers. The following list covers key books on Dracula and Bram Stoker.

Belford, Barbara. *Bram Stoker: A Biography of the Author of Dracula*
Alfred A. Knopf, New York; Weidenfeld & Nicolson, 1996

Dalby, Richard. *Bram Stoker: A Bibliography of First Editions*
Dracula Press, London, 1993

Farson, Daniel. *The Man Who Wrote Dracula: A Biography of Bram Stoker*
Michael Joseph, London, 1975

Florescu, Radu & Raymond T. McNally. *The Essential Dracula*
Mayflower Books, New York, 1979

Dracula: A Biography of Vlad the Impaler
Hawthorn Books, New York, 1973; Robert Hale & Co, London, 1974

In Search of Dracula
Graphic Society, New York, 1972; New English Library, London, 1973

Glut, Donald F. *The Dracula Book*
Scarecrow Press, New Jersey, 1975

Haining, Peter. *The Dracula Scrapbook*
Chancellor Press, London, 1987, 1992

Haining, Peter & Tremayne, Peter. *The Un-Dead; The Legend of Bram Stoker and Dracula*
Constable, London, 1997

Leatherdale, Clive. *The Origins of Dracula*
William Kimber, London, 1987

Dracula: The Novel and the Legend
Aquarian Press, Northamptonshire, 1985

Ludlum, Harry. *A Biography of Dracula: The Life Story of Bram Stoker*
Foulsham, London, 1962

Melton, J. Gordon. *The Vampire Book: The Encyclopedia of the Undead*
Visible Ink Press, Detroit, 1994

Roth, Phyllis A. *Bram Stoker*
Twayne Publishers, Boston, 1982

Shepard, Leslie. *The Dracula Book of Great Vampire Stories*
Citadel Press, New Jersey, 1977

Shepard, Leslie. *Bram Stoker, Irish Theatre Manager & Author, with information on where to visit the Dublin locations associated with Bram Stoker*
Impact Publications, Dublin, Eire, 1994

Skal, David J. (ed.). *Dracula, The Ultimate Illustrated Edition of the World Famous Vampire Play*
Hamilton Deane & John L Balderston, St. Martin's Press, New York, 1993

Stoker, Bram. *Dracula*
first published by Archibald Constable & Co, London, 1897. A first edition of the book is a rare and expensive collector's item, but the book has been reprinted continually in various editions for a century. Modern editions have been issued by Penguin Books, Brandon, Wordsworth, Everyman (J.M. Dent), Oxford University Press (World Classic series) and W. Foulsham. The Everyman edition contains useful editorial material, and the Foulsham edition also includes full text of Stoker's *The Lair of the White Worm*, and a note by Bram Stoker for the Icelandic edition of *Dracula*.

Dracula's Guest and Other Weird Stories
George Routledge & Sons, London, 1914; Brandon, Eire, 1990.

Wolf, Leonard. *The Annotated Dracula*
Clarkson N. Potter, New York, 1975; New English Library, London, 1976.